"Jack Levison has been an inspiration  a distance since I was hooked by his t began to obtain all of Jack's titles and his insights on participating in the life the indwelling Spirit of God. His newest work, *Seven Secrets of the Spirit-Filled Life*, only adds to the appreciation I have for his profound yet accessible insights into participation in the triune life. Take the 49 chapters you now hold in your hand and let Jack be a servant of the paraclete and guide you into the flow of the Spirit's transformative, therapeutic presence."

Dr. Mark J. Chironna, bishop protector,
Order of St. Maximus; founding and lead pastor,
Church On The Living Edge

"With wit, insight and clarity, Jack Levison speaks to Christians young and old who yearn for a sense of connection to God. Drawing from the Bible, Christian tradition and everyday life, Levison shows us secrets that can help us kindle (or rekindle) fervor and hope in our Christian discipleship."

Susan R. Garrett, professor of New Testament,
Louisville Presbyterian Theological Seminary

"Jack both thinks clearly and longs deeply for spirit-life. He teaches us that where there is a deep experience of the divine, the sincere pursuit of virtue and an acceleration of growth, the Spirit of God is vibrantly present. In this book Jack (and his son!) give us concrete, accessible, actionable help in the most important challenge of human living. Get ready to breathe deep."

John Ortberg, founder, BecomeNew.Me

SEVEN SECRETS
OF THE
SPIRIT-FILLED
LIFE

SEVEN SECRETS

OF THE

SPIRIT-FILLED

LIFE

Daily Renewal, Purpose and Joy When
You Partner *with the* Holy Spirit

JACK LEVISON

Chosen
a division of Baker Publishing Group
Minneapolis, Minnesota

Text © 2023 by Jack Levison
Photographs © 2023 by Jeremy Pope-Levison

Published by Chosen Books
Minneapolis, Minnesota
www.chosenbooks.com

Chosen Books is a division of
Baker Publishing Group, Grand Rapids, Michigan

Printed in the United States of America

ISBN 978-0-8007-6270-4 (trade paper)
ISBN 978-1-4934-3767-2 (ebook)
ISBN 978-0-8007-6333-6 (casebound)

Library of Congress Cataloging-in-Publication Control Number: 2022049469

Cover design by Studio Gearbox

Baker Publishing Group publications use paper produced from sustainable forestry practices and post-consumer waste whenever possible.

23 24 25 26 27 28 29   7 6 5 4 3 2 1

CONTENTS

INTRODUCTION

On my first day of college, I trekked up three flights of stairs in Wheaton College's Blanchard Hall. I sat down with 34 other students and waited—until a red-haired, middle-aged man in tortoiseshell glasses and a three-piece gray wool suit walked in, set his briefcase on the desk, opened it, turned without a word to the chalkboard and wrote something in Greek on it. Then he turned toward the class, and with a sheepish grin and playful eyes, asked, "Who knows what this means?" Well, it was the first day of Greek class, and none of us could read a word of what he'd written. So he said, "This is Philippians 4:13. Who knows what it says?" Because this was Wheaton College, nearly every student in the class raised a hand. "I can do all things through Christ who strengthens me!" we said in near unison.

Even more playfully, yet with a more serious look, too, the professor asked us, "Is this true? Can you do all things through Christ who strengthens you? Can you pass a chemistry exam without studying because Christ strengthens you? Can you run a mile without training because Christ strengthens you?" No, suggested Dr. Gerald Hawthorne, you can't, try as you might. But you can "face all things through the One who gives you power." *That* we can do.

Jerry went on to explain different philosophies of translation—literal versus dynamic equivalent, the difference between translating words versus translating concepts, and of course, the difference between translations like the New International Version, in which the class had memorized Philippians 4:13 (I can *do* all this), and the translation he had done from the original Greek (I can *face* all things). I'm beginning with this recollection because of how powerfully Jerry reframed, refreshed and revitalized the meaning of a Bible verse I thought I knew and had taken to heart.

This is what I crave for you as you read, study and pray through this book: that sense of refreshment I felt on that autumn day in 1974. It's what I've hoped and dreamed and worked for through decades of college and seminary teaching. There is so much insight to be gotten from the Bible, some of it supporting what we already believe but much of it upending what we already believe. You'll find both sorts of insight in the days ahead, and I hope you'll be open to new insight each day.

<hr>

Now for some advice about how to use this book. For starters, it contains 49 short chapters because the Jewish feast of Pentecost occurs fifty days after Passover. It would be very easy to read one chapter a day for 49 days. Why is that important? The earliest followers of Jesus, Luke tells us in the New Testament book of Acts, were filled with the Holy Spirit on the day of Pentecost. So the day after you complete the 49th chapter can be *your* Pentecost.

But don't feel obligated to finish this book in 49 days. The purpose of this book is renewal, purpose and joy. In fact, instead of working through *Seven Secrets of the Spirit-filled Life* in 49 days, you may want to go through it in about a year. That's one chapter a week. This works well because the applications aren't always easy, and you may want to practice one application for a week so it becomes a regular part of your spiritual life.

There are seven sections in this book, each highlighting one secret of Spirit-filled living. Notice that chapters for each secret have their own rhythm.

- In the first chapter of every section—chapters 1, 8, 15, 22, 29, 36 and 43—you'll be asked to breathe. That's because the Hebrew word translated in the Old Testament as Spirit is *ruach*, which often means breath. But not just breath. Never *just* breath. Breath—a steady pulse, lungs rising and falling, as we'll see—is the bedrock of the Spirit-filled life. When we breathe, we make room for renewal, we make space for discovery of purpose, we experience the respite of joy.

* The second through sixth chapters of each section contain writing on a given secret. There's a progression to these seven secrets. They begin with your individual experience of the Spirit-filled life, branch out to include the Christians around you and the world God wants to transform through you, and end with the legacy you can leave to the next generation. Yet this progression doesn't mean you need to read these in order. Feel free to dip in anywhere; I hope any chapter in any order will offer you plenty of insight to experience renewal, purpose and joy.

* On the last chapter of every section—days 7, 14, 21, 28, 35, 42 and 49—we'll reflect on a photograph rather than a biblical passage. Take your time with these photos. They are beautiful, yes, but they also capture the meaning of the previous chapters in that section. Think of this last chapter of each section as a breather—matching the first chapter of each section, when you'll actually take time to breathe—a chance to imagine a Spirit-filled life rich with renewal, purpose and joy.

The photograph at the start of this introduction—there will be seven more—represents the path you are about to take. Picture yourself standing at the start. Take whatever you need—a bottle of water, an energy bar, insect repellent (mosquitos swarmed Jeremy as he took photographs on this path!)—or more practical for your setting, no doubt, a pen, a journal, a cup of tea or coffee, a friend. Before you take a step, smell the fresh scent of the forest. Listen for birdsong. Then walk slowly. Think of the path as what I've put into this book—Bible passages, inspirational words, applications and prayers. But look, too, beyond the path to what you may discover there, outside of what I've written, because the Holy Spirit is all around, often in unexpected and unfamiliar places.

As you read, finally, I pray the Holy Spirit will transport you far beyond your expectations to a world in which you can face anything through the One who strengthens you.

ANTICIPATE INFINITELY MORE

*Discover the Holy Spirit
in your everyday life*

1

Breathe the breath of praise

By the word of the LORD the heavens were made, and all the host of them by the breath of His mouth.

—Psalm 33:6 NKJV

Praise is beautiful on the tongues of the upright. That's how I would translate the second line in Psalm 33:1. In *The Message*, it reads, "Right-living people sound best when praising." But praise doesn't come naturally to most of us. Most of us find it much easier to express hard-edged criticism, shrill judgments, relentless complaints. These roll easily off our tongues. But affirmation? Admiration? Acclaim? Not so much. That's why praise requires practice, and it's a practice we cultivate moment by moment, day to day.

God, in Psalm 33, gives us a model for practicing praise: "By the word of the LORD the heavens were made, and all the host of them by the breath of His mouth" (verse 6). The word *breath* is actually the Hebrew word *ruach*, which can be translated as Spirit and wind. It's an amazingly broad-shouldered Hebrew word that requires more than one word in English to translate it: Spirit-breath, Spirit-wind, Spirit-God. In this psalm, God created with a word when the Spirit-breath spoke life into existence, or again, in *The Message*, "The skies were made by GOD's command; he breathed the word and the stars popped out" (verse 6).

We didn't create the universe, but we can mirror that creative act by tracing it in praise. If God's Spirit-breath spoke the world into being, God's Spirit-breath within us can flow in praise for God's creation. No, we are not the Creator, but that same Spirit-breath can roll over our tongues, too.

This sort of praise is not an end in itself. It sets God—and humans—in their proper places. The poet goes on to say that God "shoots down the world's power-schemes" (Psalm 33:10 MESSAGE). On this, then, our first day together, we've learned how the Spirit-filled life begins with the praise of a powerful Creator, who puts our fragile human lives into their proper perspective.

Knowing that *ruach* is Spirit-breath, *God's* breath in you, breathe in and out deeply for one minute, at this, the start of week one. (Set a timer, if need be.) Each time you breathe out, say simply, "I praise you, God." In this way, let words of praise roll over your tongue.

> *Holy Spirit,*
>> *You breathed a word of creation through God's lips*
>> *and set the world on a solid foundation*
>> *Breathe now a word of praise through my lips*
>> *and set my world on a solid footing. Amen.*

2

Practice in secret

And Pharaoh said to his servants, "Can we find such a one
as this, a man in whom is the Spirit of God?" Then Pharaoh
said to Joseph, "Inasmuch as God has shown you all this,
there is no one as discerning and wise as you."

—Genesis 41:38–39 NKJV

When the most powerful man in the world called, they
ran—literally hustled—Joseph out of the dungeon (Genesis 41:14). He quickly shaved, changed his clothes and
appeared before the Egyptian pharaoh. Pharaoh told him
some disturbing dreams that his own magicians couldn't
unravel. But Joseph could: Seven years of plenty would be
followed by seven years of famine. What Joseph did next

is the kicker. He told Pharaoh what to do: store up food during the fat years to distribute it during the lean years. Good, practical, healthy advice for how to run a nation.

Stunned, Pharaoh asked, "Can we find such a one as this, a man in whom is the Spirit of God?" Then he answered his own question: "Inasmuch as God has shown you all this, there is no one as discerning and wise as you." In the original Hebrew, the parallel between Pharaoh's question and answer is unavoidable. Is there anyone with the Spirit *like him*? There is no one wise *like you*!

When he saw how Joseph possessed practical wisdom, Pharaoh grasped the connection: Joseph was wise because he had God's Spirit in him. Spirit and practical wisdom are joined at the hip. But how? How did Joseph come to be full of God's Spirit? By spending his life practicing, his years preparing.

In the course of his years in Egypt, Joseph had been in charge, not only of the house of Potiphar, the captain of the palace guard, but also in the prison into which he was thrown on false charges. Joseph served so well over both that neither Potiphar nor the chief jailer had to pay any attention to what lay under Joseph's care (Genesis 39:6; 39:23). Then, at just the right moment, he applied this practical wisdom to save countless men and women from starvation.

The first secret of the Spirit-filled life is that it takes shape in those invisible, unremarkable days when the Holy Spirit seems absent. It takes shape in a home, an office cubicle, a factory, even an Egyptian dungeon. If we want to lead a Spirit-filled life, we, like Joseph, must practice hard-won wisdom when no one is looking.

....

Identify one act today of practical wisdom you can do in your home or workplace or wherever you have responsibilities, knowing now that the Spirit and wisdom are joined at the hip. This might be as simple as getting in the habit of baking cookies for a neighbor in need or practicing the art of writing a note of encouragement to someone you haven't seen in ages. Whatever you do, perform that act with care and carefulness, trusting that the Holy Spirit is present and active.

> *Holy Spirit,*
>> *When no one is looking, through run-on days*
>> *Let me believe that practical wisdom matters*
>>> *sensible skills*
>>> *time-tested abilities*
>> *So that when I am called upon, I will be ready. Amen.*

3

Be filled with the Spirit of wisdom

So you shall speak to all who are gifted artisans, whom I have filled with the spirit of wisdom, that they may make Aaron's garments, to consecrate him, that he may minister to Me as priest.

—Exodus 28:3 NKJV

God gave these instructions to Moses in the middle of the desert after the Israelites experienced centuries of slavery in Egypt. Their imaginations were deadened, their hopes largely dashed.

God wanted them to anticipate infinitely more. But how?

By giving them a creative task. God wanted the artisans to spin and dye and stitch and embroider spectacular clothing for Aaron the priest so he could serve in the tabernacle, a portable tent of worship that would travel with them throughout their difficult and dry days in the desert. A bright spot, colorful and vibrant, against the monotonous tan backdrop of the wilderness.

The artisans were gifted. This word, *gifted*, is literally in Hebrew, *wise*-of-heart. The wise of heart, artisans with practical skills—weaving, spinning, dyeing—were filled with the Spirit of *wisdom*. *Wise* and *wisdom* go hand in hand. *Skill* and *Spirit* are joined at the hip.

But there's more. The artisans didn't just have dribs and drabs of the Spirit. God *filled* them. The Hebrew verb here means *filled to overflowing*. Houses during the plagues in Egypt were filled—*infested*—with flies (Exodus 8:21). When the Jordan River filled its banks, it *flooded* (Joshua 3:15). In the same way, when the time came, the artisans rolled up their sleeves and went to work, since they were overflowing with the Spirit of wisdom.

How does this happen? It can be simple. For example, my wife, Priscilla, who loves to spin and knit, began a prayer shawl-knitting group in our church in Seattle. The group gathered monthly to knit shawls for seriously ill people in the hospital. After blessing the shawls in a church service, the group hand-delivered them personally.

Or maybe you built a house alongside a family that could never afford one otherwise. You painted walls, hooked up wiring, installed plumbing. And there it is: beauty in the desert, carved out by modern-day artisans filled with the Spirit of wisdom.

––––––––––

Practice one skill today, however small it may seem at the moment. While you do, anticipate infinitely more a time when God will call you to practice that skill, perhaps with others, in a lavish act of generosity.

> *Holy Spirit,*
>> *No skill is too small, no task too routine*
>>> *To escape you*
>> *So fill me to overflowing with practical wisdom*
>>> *With wisdom practiced for others. Amen.*

4

Say *No!* to distractions

Now when Balaam saw that it pleased the LORD to bless Israel, he did not resort to divination as at other times, but turned his face toward the wilderness. When Balaam looked out and saw Israel encamped tribe by tribe, the Spirit of God came on him.

—Numbers 24:1–2 NIV

Balaam was a Babylonian seer who made his living by divination. He was renowned for discovering the future in patterns produced by the smoke of sacrificed animals or the lines in their livers. He was the first choice for Balak, king of Moab, an enemy of Israel, who offered to pay him handsomely to predict doom for the Israelites.

Yet Israel's God made clear from the start, even through the mouth of Balaam's talking donkey, that this wouldn't be easy because Israel was a blessed nation. Cursing Israel just wouldn't do.

Still, Balaam pressed on. Twice, he sacrificed seven bulls and rams, no doubt to see what the smoke and innards would tell him. And both times God told him, without smoke and livers, to bless Israel.

Only on the third go-round did Balaam see infinitely more. Why? Because only then did Balaam "not resort to divination as at other times." No more smoke or livers. Balaam put all of that aside.

Then, and only then, did his priorities change forever. Having given up the distraction of divination, Balaam received the Spirit and saw God face-to-face. Everything else faded away, and he became "a man with 20/20 vision . . . who hears God speak . . . who falls on his face in worship, who sees what's really going on" (Numbers 24:3–4 MESSAGE).

Sometimes it's not what we do that paves the way for the Spirit, but what we *don't* do. For Balaam, this was divination. Only when he put that practice aside did he receive the Spirit and see God.

Sure, Balaam got it right about Israel all three times. But there is a big difference between knowing the truth and knowing the God of Truth, between seeing what will happen and seeing the One who makes life happen. Only when the Spirit came upon him during the third go-round was Balaam taken completely aback *by God*. And that occurred only when he put aside the distraction that stood in the way.

Identify one distraction in your life today that keeps you from the Spirit-filled opportunity to see God face-to-face. This could be anything, such as too much time spent on social media—really, anything that distracts you from living the Spirit-filled life to the full. Devise a plan to phase this distraction out of your life.

> *Holy Spirit,*
> > *It's not curls of smoke that keep me from seeing God*
> > > *But my own cherished habits*
> > > *my own prized practices that hold me back.*
> > *Today, Holy Spirit,*
> > > *Inspire me to end them*
> > > *Stir me to stop them in their tracks. Amen.*

5

Wait—*actively*

When the day of Pentecost came, they were all together in one place. Suddenly a sound like the blowing of a violent wind came from heaven and filled the whole house where they were sitting. They saw what seemed to be tongues of fire that separated and came to rest on each of them. All of them were filled with the Holy Spirit and began to speak in other tongues as the Spirit enabled them. Now there were staying in Jerusalem God-fearing Jews from every nation under heaven.

—Acts 2:1–5 NIV

The drama of Pentecost—a rushing wind, fiery tongues and miraculous speech—happened *suddenly* (Acts 2:2). But all of a sudden doesn't mean as a surprise. Peter even explained that the prophet Joel had described these strange happenings centuries earlier (Acts 2:16–21). How did Peter know what to expect? He and everyone with him had spent weeks preparing for just this moment.

Jesus had given clear instructions: "Do not leave Jerusalem, but wait for the gift my Father promised" (Acts 1:4). So they settled down and waited. The roomful of Jesus' followers, men and women, was so serious about taking Jesus at his word, they didn't even stay at the Mount of Olives. It would have been easier—and more spiritual—for them to bend the rules a bit and sleep in the shadow of Jesus' ascension. They didn't. They trudged three miles to Jerusalem and waited, away from the fray of a miracle-fed faith.

They waited, but not idly. Jesus' disciples "all joined together constantly in prayer, along with the women and Mary the mother of Jesus, and with his brothers" (Acts 1:14). Jesus' earliest followers prayed together. *A lot.*

And they studied. We know this from what the onlookers said: "We hear them declaring the wonders of God in our own tongues!" (Acts 2:11). The phrase *wonders of God* is shorthand for God's mighty acts throughout history. Moses told the Israelites to acknowledge God's wonders (Deuteronomy 11:2), and Psalm 105:1–2 begins with encouragement to sing praises by reciting the wonders of God. With all the talk of tongues and fire and drunks at 9 a.m., we tend to miss this: Jesus' people studied Scripture so that, when the time came, they were ready to recite the wonders of God.

On the face of it, the drama of Pentecost seems entirely unexpected. It wasn't. Left alone, Jesus' family, friends and followers waited, prayed and studied. And once they did, all Pentecost broke loose!

Read slowly through one of the Old Testament passages Peter recited at Pentecost, trying to imagine the amazement Jesus' followers felt as they discovered his story and theirs in these chapters. Choose from Joel 2 (Acts 2:16–21), Psalm 16 (Acts 2:25–28), Psalm 110 (Acts 2:34) and Isaiah 57 (Peter quotes Isaiah 57:19 briefly in Acts 2:39). Write a small section of whatever passage you choose somewhere—on your bathroom mirror, in your phone or on a sheet of paper—so that you can recite it regularly as you anticipate infinitely more of the Spirit-filled life.

> *Holy Spirit,*
>> *Train me to wait*
>> *Teach me to pray*
>> *Tutor me to study*
>> *So that I can begin to anticipate infinitely more. Amen.*

6

Ponder the vision

While Peter was still thinking about the vision, the Spirit said to him, "Simon, three men are looking for you. So get up and go downstairs. Do not hesitate to go with them, for I have sent them."

—Acts 10:19–20 NIV

Peter was tired and hungry. He had preached at Pentecost, healed a man, gone to jail, defended himself in the Jewish senate, led a church with lots of growth, paid a visit to Samaria and survived a persecution. Yes, Peter was tired and hungry.

Still, at noon, he trudged up the steps to the roof of a house and prayed (Acts 10:9). That's significant. No. That's *essential*. Peter found a quiet place and prayed.

33

On that roof, Peter had a vision of unclean, non-kosher foods descending in a picnic blanket three times. Twice he refused to eat. He finally realized, on the third go-round, that he was not supposed to discriminate between kosher and non-kosher food—between kosher and non-kosher *people* (Acts 10:10–16).

What Peter did next is vital to the Spirit-filled life. He didn't revel in the vision. He didn't run downstairs and tell everyone, even though that would have raised his stature in the church. He certainly didn't say, "Well, that was amazing worship. I'm famished. Let's eat!"

Instead, Peter puzzled over the vision (Acts 10:17). He chewed on it. Fretted it, the way a dog frets a bone. This was not a spectacle to be broadcast; it was an urgent message to be obeyed.

Even when guests came to the door, he didn't run downstairs to meet them, despite an ancient Jewish guarantee of hospitality. He stayed on the roof to think through the vision.

Then, and only then, did the Spirit speak to Peter, "while Peter was still thinking about the vision."

In this story, the Spirit didn't prompt Peter to pray or inspire his vision or cause him to puzzle over its meaning. All of these occurred *before* the Spirit spoke to Peter. This combination of prayer, vision and contemplation were essential practices that led Peter to the point at which he could hear the Spirit speak.

....

Identify one practice you think will be most effective to set yourself in a place to hear the Holy Spirit. Devise simple strategies to ensure that you keep up this practice.

> *Holy Spirit,*
>> *When I'm*
>>> *too tired to pray*
>>> *too tired to wonder*
>>> *too tired to think*
>> *Meet me there, even when*
>>> *my prayer is rote*
>>> *my curiosity dim*
>>> *my mind weary*
>> *I'll wait. I'll listen. I'll hear. Amen.*

7

Reflect on the promise of infinitely more

The Holy Spirit can come to us unexpectedly. My mother told the story of a brutal argument she had with my father before he was a Christian. While he was still in bed, she left for church, barking, "He's all yours, God." For some reason, my father showed up in church that morning. And, as he told the story, he felt someone—the Holy Spirit—shove him from behind (my father wasn't given to gentle nudges), so he walked up the short aisle and committed his life to Christ. Funny thing. My mother sang a solo that day, so we have this all on tape—one of those little cassette tapes from the seventies. You can even hear the splash of water during my dad's baptism.

Yes, the Holy Spirit can come unexpectedly, but the Spirit-filled life itself is a lifelong effort to experience the Spirit more fully *every single day*. Some Christians call this sanctification, others discipleship. Eugene Peterson names it *A Long Obedience in the Same Direction*. Whatever we call it, we know there's more to the Spirit-filled life, more filling to the brim, fullness to overflowing, awaiting us.

That fullness takes practice. The practice of praise. Practice in secret, when no one is looking. Practice in practical skills, like sewing or cooking or painting. Practice in prayer. Practice in pausing to ponder.

Today's photograph captures the power of practice with a spinner (who just happens to be *my* favorite spinner, Priscilla). Notice the gentle curve of her skilled hand, the whirl of the bobbin—or whatever else attracts your attention. Pause over this aspect of the photograph as you ponder practices that let you discover the Holy Spirit in your everyday life.

This, then, is the first secret of the Spirit-filled life: *When we practice—anything from praise to prayer, administration to meditation, carving to cooking—we open ourselves more and more to the Holy Spirit.*

Today, as you reflect upon the skill of this spinner, ask yourself these questions:

* What *unhelpful* habit or distraction do I need to put aside to discover the Spirit in my everyday life?
* What *beneficial* practice do I need to cultivate to discover the Spirit in my everyday life?
* What *new* practice do I need to begin to discover the Spirit in my everyday life?

Then devise a practical plan, for one day at least, to put one unhelpful habit or distraction aside, to foster one beneficial practice and to incorporate one new practice. Write this plan down wherever you will see it as you go through your day.

> *Holy Spirit,*
> > *Help me to live for the long haul*
> > *To set aside what hampers*
> > *To pick up what helps*
> > *To practice—and practice some more   the skills that*
> > > *make room for you*
> > > *in everyday life. Amen.*

SATURATE
YOURSELF WITH
SCRIPTURE

*Discover how the Bible
nourishes the Spirit-filled life*

8

Breathe the breath of integrity

As long as my breath is in me and the spirit of God is in my nostrils, my lips will not speak falsehood, and my tongue will not utter deceit.

—Job 27:3–4 NRSV

At the start of each week, we go back to basics because the bedrock of the Spirit-filled life is *ruach*, nothing more—and nothing less—than Spirit-breath. This Spirit-breath is with us moment by moment as a precious gift, a prized source of life. If we pay attention to this Spirit-breath, we won't easily take for granted life itself in our desire for more. Sometimes, appreciating what we have rather than striving for more is the path to fullness of life.

Nowhere is this more visible than in the biblical book of Job, which preserves poignant thoughts about sorrow, loss and God's responsibility for suffering. Job, a figure of epic proportion for all he lost—his home, his children and his health—occupied an infamous ash heap, where he sat along the razor-sharp edge between life and death. Where better to appreciate the Spirit-breath, which gives life, than in the shadow of death?

This *ruach* is a wonderful blend of human breath and divine Spirit. In today's passage, Job himself parallels *breath* in him with the *Spirit* of God in his nostrils (and I'd capitalize Spirit here!). Spirit-breath pulses in us, Job knew, especially when we inhabit the heart of darkness, when all we have left is the ability to breathe.

Back to basics.

That's why Job used the phrase *as long as*. He knew the limits of life—*as long as*. He knew the certainty of death—*as long as*. But he knew, too, that the Spirit-breath thrived in him, if only for a short time, a sliver of eternity.

And what does that Spirit-breath bring? Integrity. Truth. Honesty. "As long as my breath is in me and the Spirit of God is in my nostrils," claimed Job, "my lips will not speak falsehood, and my tongue will not utter deceit."

Truth doesn't always dazzle. Honesty doesn't always astound. But these provide bedrock evidence, exhibit A, of the Spirit-filled life.

43

Knowing that *ruach* is Spirit-breath, *God's* breath in you, breathe in and out deeply for two minutes at this, the start of week two. (Set a timer, if need be.) Each time you breathe in, say, "Keep me honest, God." Each time you breathe out, state what you want to be honest about. For example, breathe in, "Keep me honest, God," and breathe out, "when I am at work." Whatever you say, practice and pray for a life of integrity, because integrity is the foundation of the Spirit-filled life.

> *Holy Spirit,*
>> *When I open my mouth and your Spirit-breath*
>> *rolls over my tongue*
>> *Keep me honest*
>> *Let my yes be yes and my no, no*
>> *Honest as long as I live*
>> *Simply honest. Amen.*

9

Study with the Spirit

You gave your good Spirit to instruct them. You did not withhold your manna from their mouths, and you gave them water for their thirst.

—Nehemiah 9:20 NIV

If you know the story of the exodus—Israel's escape from Egypt—you may know the story of manna, a bread-like dew that appeared every morning in the wilderness to nourish the Israelites, who had only recently escaped from Egypt. You may also know the story of miraculous, tasty water. The water was bitter, but when Moses hit a rock with his stick, out bubbled sweet water instead.

Today's passage about Spirit, manna and water is followed by a sweeping recollection of God's sustenance: "For forty years you sustained them in the wilderness; they lacked nothing, their clothes did not wear out nor did their feet become swollen" (Nehemiah 9:21).

But manna and water were not all God gave them. God also gave them his good Spirit to instruct them. Is anything as vital as water, as essential as bread, in a desert? Yes! Learning was as important as manna and water, and learning demanded a great Teacher—God's good Spirit.

That good Spirit *instructed* the Israelites. *Instruct* is a powerful word in Hebrew. In Nehemiah 8:13, just a chapter earlier, the people had "gathered around Ezra the teacher to give attention to the words of the Law." The same Hebrew word translated *instruct* in Nehemiah 9:20 is translated *give attention to* in Ezra 8:13. We need to *pay attention* to the Bible.

Learning is no less vital, no less essential to the Spirit-filled life, than satisfying hunger and thirst. Therefore, God gave all three—manna, water *and Spirit*—to nourish and teach them.

Jesus understood this perfectly. While he was deep in conversation one afternoon with a Samaritan woman about springs of living water, the disciples were concerned that he hadn't eaten. They were puzzled when he replied, "My food is to do the will of him who sent me and to finish his work" (John 4:34). Jesus, it seems, *paid attention* to what mattered.

46

Do some basic calculations today. First, keep track of how many minutes you dedicate to eating and drinking. (This can include shopping, preparing, eating, drinking and cleaning up afterward.) Next, keep track of how many minutes you dedicate to giving careful attention to the Bible. Third, compare these numbers. If you would like to adjust them, how would you want these numbers to look tomorrow?

> *Holy Spirit,*
> *I love the scent of fresh bread*
>   *the sparkle of ice-cold water on my parched tongue*
> *But don't satisfy my hunger completely—keep me*
>   *famished for learning*
> *Don't quench my thirst entirely—keep me*
>   *longing for wisdom*
> *Teach me to pay attention*
>   *while I saturate myself with Scripture. Amen.*

10

Drink deep of ageless visions

> And behold, there was a man in Jerusalem whose name was
> Simeon, and this man was just and devout, waiting for the
> Consolation of Israel, and the Holy Spirit was upon him.
> And it had been revealed to him by the Holy Spirit that he
> would not see death before he had seen the Lord's Christ.
> So he came by the Spirit into the temple.
>
> —Luke 2:25–27 NKJV

When Jesus' parents, Joseph and Mary, brought their son
to be dedicated at the temple, no one apparently paid much
attention. But one old woman, Anna, and one old man,
Simeon, recognized the significance in the son of Mary and

Joseph! Today's passage is clear: This acute awareness was the work of the Holy Spirit on the fringes of society. The Holy Spirit was on Simeon, revealed the significance of Jesus to him and guided him. That's *three* ways of describing the Spirit-filled life.

Why was Simeon so open to the Spirit? Because he awaited the Consolation of Israel. This means he looked for the comfort promised in the Old Testament in Isaiah 40:1–2, which begins, "Comfort, yes, comfort My people!"

Isaiah 40:1–2, in fact, begins a section extending from Isaiah chapter 40 through Isaiah 55. If what Simeon went on to say to Jesus' parents were a jigsaw puzzle, each piece would be a snippet of Isaiah 40–55.

- Simeon's prayer about salvation, "which you have prepared in the sight of all nations" (Luke 2:31 NIV) mirrors Isaiah 52:10: "The LORD will lay bare his holy arm in the sight of all the nations" (NIV).
- Simeon's knowledge that Jesus would be "a light to bring revelation to the Gentiles" (Luke 2:32) comes from Isaiah 42:6, "I will keep You and give You . . . as a light to the Gentiles."
- Simeon's belief that Jesus was the "glory of Your people Israel" (Luke 2:32) echoes Isaiah 46:13: "And I will place salvation in Zion, for Israel My glory."

What came out of Simeon's Spirit-filled mouth when he saw Jesus? A Scripture-laced promise acknowledging the future impact of Jesus. With the Holy Spirit upon him, Simeon recognized the ageless vision he'd read, read and read some more: the salvation of God for all nations now in a Nazarene baby brought to the temple by peasant parents, two turtledoves in tow.

In any translation you choose, commit to memory a verse or two from the ageless vision of Isaiah 40–55. Write them down, perhaps on your phone or a small piece of paper. Carry them with you. Recite them at key moments throughout your day—and one last time by heart as you end your day.

> *Holy Spirit,*
> > *Lead me not to new revelations—but to old*
> > > *not to novel visions—but to ageless ones*
> > *Only when I've learned the past, lead me to the future.*
> > *Amen.*

11

Remember your first faith

The Friend, the Holy Spirit whom the Father will send at my request, will make everything plain to you. He will remind you of all the things I have told you.

—John 14:26 MESSAGE

During his final hours on earth, Jesus did a lot to explain what the Holy Spirit would do after he left. The Holy Spirit, Jesus explained, would make everything plain by reminding his followers of all that he had told them while he walked among them.

With almost no time left, then, Jesus emphasized that the Holy Spirit would commit less to providing new revelations than to unpacking the deeper meaning of his life, death and resurrection. The Spirit would be preoccupied less with revealing the future than revealing the past—*Jesus'* past.

This is exactly what the Holy Spirit did. The Spirit illuminated Jesus' words and actions by reminding his followers of everything he said and did.

Maybe, for example, you remember how Jesus rode into Jerusalem on a donkey. John, in his gospel, explains, "The disciples didn't notice the fulfillment of many Scriptures at the time, but after Jesus was glorified, they remembered that what was written about him matched what was done to him" (John 12:16). What was written? Zechariah 9:9, in the Old Testament: "Lo, your king comes to you . . . humble and riding on a donkey" (NRSV).

The fingerprints of the Holy Spirit are all over this. While he was still alive, Jesus' friends couldn't understand the meaning of his entry into Jerusalem on a donkey. But after his death, *the Friend, the Holy Spirit,* made everything plain by reminding them of all the things Jesus had told them. They came to this inspired understanding of Jesus' puzzling action while they studied the Old Testament—passages such as Zechariah 9:9.

This hunger to learn all about Jesus—about Jesus' *past*—energized the earliest Christians. It can energize us, too, with four gospels to occupy us in lifelong study, and a reliable Teacher, the Friend, the Holy Spirit, who will unpack for us the meaning of all Jesus said and did.

Read John 12:12–16 in light of Zechariah 9:9–10. Reflect for a few moments on what the king will bring in Zechariah 9:10. Find one concrete way today you can extend this promise of peace to the people around you.

> *Holy Spirit,*
>> *Teacher, Friend, Reminder*
>> *Tear me from the worry of tomorrow*
>> *Root me in the past*
>>> *your past*
>> *so that I can shape tomorrow today*
>>>> *your way. Amen.*

12

Learn the Bible from Jesus

Then Peter, filled with the Holy Spirit, said to them, "Rulers of the people and elders of Israel."

—Acts 4:8 NKJV

Just because they healed a man, John and Peter were arrested, jailed and trotted out the next morning for their trial in front of, as *The Message* puts it, "everybody who was anybody." Tough audience.

Thankfully, the Holy Spirit filled Peter, who launched into a defense. But his defense is surprisingly short. *Really* short. It's a Scripture sandwich—two lines about Jesus connected by Psalm 118:22: the "stone which was rejected by you builders, which has become the chief cornerstone" (Acts 4:11 KJV).

Now the words at the beginning, he was "filled with the Holy Spirit," might lead us to think that the psalm came to Peter all of a sudden, out of the blue. It didn't.

Psalm 118:22 was well-known among early Christians. In 1 Peter 2:1–10, it occurs alongside other Old Testament verses as part of a list that early Christians probably memorized. Psalm 118:22, then, did not occur to Peter in a flash of inspiration. When the Holy Spirit filled him, this verse came out of his mouth. Out of his *memory*, really.

The leaders' response gives us another clue to how Peter knew this psalm: "Now when they saw the boldness of Peter and John, and perceived that they were uneducated and untrained men, they marveled. And they realized that they had been with Jesus" (Acts 4:13).

The hearers realized Peter and John had been with Jesus. How so? Because Peter referred to exactly the same verse, Psalm 118:22, that Jesus had quoted in his story of the wicked tenants (Mark 12:10 11; Matthew 21:42; Luke 20:17). Peter used the same psalm in the same way that Jesus did—to explain Jesus' death.

In the Spirit-filled life, then, education and inspiration, the Spirit and study, go hand in glove, causing even the toughest souls to recognize that we have been with Jesus.

Jesus and his earliest followers cherished the Old Testament psalms. Read Psalm 1 today, not only because it is the first in the book of Psalms, but also because this psalm is about learning. Read verses 2–3 slowly. In verse 2, what is the source of delight? In verse 3, what images describe the impact of a life of learning? Come up with one strategy for being a Spirit-filled student of Scripture whom others would describe as a well-nourished tree.

> *Holy Spirit,*
> *Inspire me to learn the words of Jesus by heart*
> *the words Jesus learned by heart*
> *So that people will know I've been with Jesus. Amen.*

13

Wait for the deep things of God

As it is written: "What no eye has seen, what no ear has heard, and what no human mind has conceived"—the things God has prepared for those who love him—these are the things God has revealed to us by his Spirit. The Spirit searches all things, even the deep things of God.

—1 Corinthians 2:9–10 NIV

When I hear the words "the things God has revealed to us by his Spirit," my mind jumps immediately to brand-new insights given directly to me out of the blue. Mysteries revealed. Problems solved. Secrets unlocked.

It may seem like there's a biblical basis for this understanding of Paul's words. In his instructions about how to worship, Paul advised the Corinthians, "If a revelation is made to someone else sitting nearby, let the first person be silent" (1 Corinthians 14:30 NRSV). Revelation here sure sounds like a *direct* revelation.

But we're nearly through week two—*Saturate yourself with Scripture*—so it won't surprise us that this isn't Paul's idea of revelation. Revelation isn't direct at all. "The things God has revealed to us by his Spirit" come through a sustained study of Scripture.

We know this, for the apostle Paul at least, because his letters are chock-full of snippets and lengthy quotations of the Old Testament (the only Bible Paul read, since the New Testament didn't exist yet). Paul's words are jam-packed with Old Testament words, phrases and sentences.

Even when he describes revelation by the Spirit, in today's passage, he adopts Old Testament language. "What no eye has seen, what no ear has heard, and what no human mind has conceived" comes straight from Isaiah 64:4, which reads, "Since ancient times no one has heard, no ear has perceived, no eye has seen any God besides you."[1] The quotation is so direct that translators put these words in quotation marks even though the original Greek manuscripts of Paul's letters didn't have quotation marks!

Paul saturated himself with Scripture. His sustained and serious study provided the fertile ground for revelation by

1. Isaiah 64:3 in the Hebrew Bible.

the Spirit. When we, like Paul, are hungry for a serious and sustained study of Scripture—both Old and New Testaments for us—we, like Paul, find ourselves on the revelation-rich journey of the Spirit-filled life.

———

The next line in Isaiah 64:4, which Paul doesn't quote in 1 Corinthians 2:9–10, reads, "who acts on behalf of those who wait for him." Take some time today to reflect upon what it means to wait for God because waiting is essential for grasping "the deep things of God," which Paul refers to in 1 Corinthians 2:9–10. The deep things of God don't come quickly or easily, without waiting, without study.

> *Holy Spirit,*
>> *When I lack focus, sharpen my sight*
>> *When I'm distracted, arrest my attention*
>> *When I want easy answers, a shortcut to revelation*
>> *Teach me to wait*
>>> *to study*
>>> *to listen*
>> *Until I'm absorbed in the deep things of God. Amen.*

14

Reflect on the Spirit and Scripture

During college, I lived in a run-down rental on the edge of campus. It was forgettable—except for the stench of six 21-year-old guys. But I remember the basement. Not because it was finished, which it wasn't. And not because it was cozy, which it wasn't. I remember that basement, with its dirt floor and crooked cement walls, because that's where I had my morning devotions.

I'd head downstairs to my makeshift desk, where I'd spend the first hour of my day doing word studies—tracing a Greek word through the New Testament. I don't remember a single word I studied or an insight I gained or a thought that came to me. But I remember the powerful sense of slipping away to study, carving out time to learn and listen, not to a professor to pass an exam, but to the Holy Spirit.

That's the image I hope you've garnered this week—slipping away to saturate yourself with Scripture. The Israelites did this; the good Spirit taught them. Simeon did this; he knew Isaiah like the back of his hand. Jesus promised that the Spirit would remind believers of his life in light of the Old Testament. Peter and Paul, both steeped in Scripture, explained how vividly the Old Testament illuminated the life of Jesus.

Today's photograph captures this love of Scripture with an ancient Hebrew scroll. Notice the careful script, then imagine the patience each letter took to copy by hand. Notice creases formed over centuries, then imagine the fingers that followed each line, right to left, as generation after generation read this scroll. Pause over this scroll and ponder your own commitment to studying Scripture slowly, to reading it meditatively, thoughtfully, carefully.

This, then, is the second secret of the Spirit-filled life: *A rich, regular study of Scripture nourishes the Spirit-filled life, leading us deeper and deeper into the core of our faith—how Jesus lived, died and rose from the dead.*

Today, as you reflect on this photograph, prepare yourself for a serious session devoted to the study of Scripture:

* Locate a place (a closet, a couch, a crawl space, or a cluster of trees) where you can step away for the study of Scripture.
* Nail down one time this coming week you can devote to the serious study of Scripture.
* Select one passage from Scripture you want to study.

As you begin, ask the Holy Spirit to help you study. A good teacher is *always* ready to help when a student wants to learn—and the Holy Spirit is nothing if not a good teacher.

> *Holy Spirit,*
> > *Teacher, Revealer, Reminder*
> > > *When I slip away to study, away from the fray*
> > > *Come by my side, shoulder to shoulder*
> > *Reminding, revealing, teaching. Amen.*

COMMIT TO COMMUNITY

*Discover the power
of the Holy Spirit alongside others*

15

Breathe the breath of creation

> If you turned your back, they'd die in a
>   minute—
> Take back your Spirit and they die, revert to
>   original mud;
> Send out your Spirit and they spring to life—
> the whole countryside in bloom and blossom.
>   —Psalm 104:29–30 MESSAGE

All of creation exists in perfect harmony. God is "beautifully, gloriously robed, dressed up in sunshine" (Psalm 104:1–2). The winds are God's messengers, springs and streams refresh the earth, storks have suitable homes, mountain goats climb, badgers burrow, sun and moon mark time, even Leviathan frolics in the ocean! "What a wildly wonderful world, GOD! You made it all, with Wisdom at your side, made earth overflow with your wonderful creations" (Psalm 104:24).

Except, that is, for death. "If you turned your back, they'd die in a minute—take back your Spirit and they die, revert to original mud." There is one crack in the foundation of God's glory. Death.

Like the serpent in the garden of Eden, death creeps into our lives uninvited. Back to mud, as in the story of the first man and woman: "You started out as dirt, you'll end up dirt" (Genesis 3:19). There's no escaping death.

But that's not the end of the story—or this psalm—is it? The pendulum swings to death, but it swings even more to life: "Send out your Spirit and they spring to life—the whole countryside in bloom and blossom."

Death is *not* the final word. And until then, we have other words. Words of praise when the Spirit-breath rolls over our tongues. Words of song, too. That's why the phrase *as long as*, which we saw at the start of last week, pops up three verses after today's passage: "Let me sing to GOD all my life long, sing hymns to my God as long as I live!" (Psalm 104:33). *As long as.*

No, I won't live forever. Death is real, a blot, a blight. But until then, *all my life long, as long as I live*, I will praise God. That is the bedrock belief of the Spirit-filled life—the Spirit-breath-filled life!

Knowing that *ruach* is Spirit-breath, *God's* breath in you, breathe in and out deeply for three minutes at this, the start of week three. (Set a timer, if need be.) Breathe out and say, "Send out your Spirit." Breathe in and say, "They spring to life," but instead of "they," substitute actual parts of God's creation. For example,

Breathe out: "Send out your Spirit-breath . . ."
Breathe in: "Golden retrievers spring to life . . ."

Breathe out: "Send out your Spirit-breath . . ."
Breathe in: "[Your name] springs to life . . ."

When you're done, reflect on how your perspective has changed. What were you focused on *before* you read today's reflection and breathed praise for three minutes? What are you focused on *now*?

> *Holy Spirit,*
> *Let me not ignore evil*
> *or pretend pain's not there*
> *or disregard death*
> *Let me praise all my life long—*
> *in the shadow of evil, pain and death*
> *As long as I breathe, be my Spirit-breath*
> *forming words of praise on my lips for this wildly*
> *wonderful world. Amen.*

16

Get ready for the promise

I will sprinkle clean water on you, and you will be clean; I will cleanse you from all your impurities and from all your idols. I will give you a new heart and put a new spirit in you; I will remove from you your heart of stone and give you a heart of flesh. And I will put my Spirit in you and move you to follow my decrees and be careful to keep my laws.

—Ezekiel 36:25–27 NIV

In junior high, I owned a *Jesus Person Pocket Promise Book*. I loved that little book. My copy was tattered and frayed. It held promise after promise to encourage me. But it didn't tell me that sometimes a promise is preceded by ruthless purging. And it didn't tell me that some promises were meant for communities—not just me.

Ezekiel's promise of a new heart and Spirit is both—realistic and communal. It comes at a time after the formidable empire of Babylon had devastated Jerusalem, Israel's main city, and sent its leading lights, the prophet Ezekiel among them, into exile far away. Ezekiel saw the wreckage: his beloved nation dazed, destroyed, distraught.

So he promised them a new heart and Spirit.

But Ezekiel wasn't naïve. God wouldn't simply plop a new heart and Spirit into Israel. Their past, Ezekiel realized, had led to this shocking present. They ignored a rift between rich and poor and allowed faith to become captive to currency, worship to the whims of the wealthy. The nation needed surgery to receive a new heart and spirit. The route to renewal is excruciating.

That's where cleansing comes in. God would purify Israel by sprinkling water over them. That might sound gentle—like fresh spring rain. It's not. The Hebrew verb *sprinkle* pictures the blood of slaughtered animals dashed against the altar in the temple. Ezekiel's nation needed water not so much sprinkled as splattered all over them.

The Message has it right: "I'll pour pure water over you and scrub you clean. I'll give you a new heart, put a new spirit in you."

We're a long way from the *Jesus Person Pocket Promise Book*. But not very far away. The promise of a new heart and Spirit is still there for our communities. Yet if we want to be a People of the Promise, we have to unite justice and worship, faith and fairmindedness. And for this, we'll need surgery—and a good scrubbing.

As you begin today to consider the Holy Spirit—a *new* Spirit—in communities, write down a promise for your church, town or nation. Then ask yourself, "What would need to be scrubbed clean to arrive at that promise?" Write that down, too, and share both with someone today.

> *Holy Spirit,*
>> *Lead us on the path to promise*
>>> *with a new heart and a new Spirit*
>> *But fortify us, too, for the pain that leads to promise*
>>> *and scrub us clean along the way. Amen.*

17

Lean into community life

So I prophesied as He commanded me, and breath came into them, and they lived, and stood upon their feet, an exceedingly great army.

—Ezekiel 37:10 NKJV

In today's passage, breath, *ruach*, swoops into a valley of very many, very dry bones. (As in yesterday's reflection, Jerusalem lies in ruins, its leaders in exile. Israel is a mound of bleached bones.) Then four winds—the same Hebrew word, *ruach*—converge in a life-giving storm of inspiration. And God promises, "I will put My Spirit in you, and you shall live" (Ezekiel 37:14). That's *ruach*, too.

Ten times, the Hebrew word *ruach* occurs rapid-fire in the prophet Ezekiel's vision of a valley of dry bones come to life (Ezekiel 37:1–14). With all this *ruach, dem bones gonna rise again!*

You won't find this explosion of *ruach* in English-language Bibles, where three different words translate the same Hebrew word, *ruach*: breath, wind and Spirit. Only in the Hebrew do you find, ten times, *ruach, ruach, ruach, ruach, ruach, ruach, ruach, ruach, ruach, ruach!*

What you will find, if you read carefully, is that these dry bones aren't just a collection of individuals, each with a private experience of the Spirit. Ezekiel was amazed: "Suddenly a rattling; and the bones came together, bone to bone" (Ezekiel 37:7). These bones "lived, and stood upon their feet, an exceedingly great army" (verse 10). There's connection here—together, bone to bone. There's community here—a huge army, *very, very!* (That's how the Hebrew reads.)

Ezekiel's vision tells us that the Spirit energizes whole communities that are bruised, broken, battered and bleached in the desert sun—bringing them together into one web of connection, one community clattering back to life. *Dem bones gonna rise again!*

That's why, in Hebrew at least, the *you* is plural—*y'all*. The Spirit-breath comes into you, *plural*. The Spirit, in short, inspires connection and community.

The Spirit-filled life does bring deeply personal experiences. But they are not meant to disconnect us *from* others or to distinguish us *above* others. They are meant to connect us *to* others—different bones in one body.

Take one small step today to mend a shattered community, perhaps one of which you are a part. Maybe a call, a text, an email or a handwritten note. Maybe a donation to an organization that helps bring communities back to life. Maybe an invitation to coffee or lunch. If the Spirit-wind-breath of God breathes new life into broken communities, then join with the Spirit, in a small but concrete way, to bring a community—*any* community—back to life.

> *Holy Spirit,*
>> *Fill me, but not in a way that isolates me from others*
>> *Move me, but not in a way that raises me above others*
>> *Stir me by connecting me to others*
>>> *Bone of my bones*
>>> *Flesh of my flesh. Amen.*

18

Become a disciplined disciple

While they were worshiping the Lord and fasting, the Holy Spirit said, "Set apart for me Barnabas and Saul for the work to which I have called them." So after they had fasted and prayed, they placed their hands on them and sent them off. The two of them, sent on their way by the Holy Spirit, went down to Seleucia and sailed from there to Cyprus.

—Acts 13:2–4 NIV

"While they were worshiping the Lord and fasting." These words tell us that community practices prepare us to receive a word of the Holy Spirit. Remember Peter praying on the roof instead of eating lunch? Now the whole church in Antioch worshiped and fasted.

This is hard work. The Greek word translated in today's passage as *worshiping* could also be translated as *serving* in practical ways, such as financial support or public service. In Paul's letter to the Romans, for example, this same verb, *leitourgein*, describes serving with an offering of money (Romans 15:27). Whatever they were doing, whether worshiping or serving or giving, the church in Antioch was hard at work.

That work also involved fasting—giving up food for a certain period of time. The earliest Christians fasted a lot. We know this from a very early Christian collection of teachings called the *Didache*. Remember Jesus' command to "pray for those who persecute you" (Matthew 5:44)? *Didache* 1:3 says to pray *and fast* for persecutors. And baptism? Both baptizer and baptized needed to fast before baptism, according to *Didache* 7:4. Christians are told, too, to fast on Wednesdays and Fridays—two days a week (8:1). That's a lot of fasting.

Fasting, worship and prayer didn't stop after the church in Antioch received a word of the Holy Spirit, which was vague, for sure. (To what *work* had the Holy Spirit called Saul and Barnabas? The Holy Spirit didn't say.)

After receiving this word, they went right back to prayer and fasting to figure out what to do. Once they figured it out, there was no fanfare, no flashy farewell. They simply laid their hands on Saul and Barnabas and let them go, sending the pair on their way by the Holy Spirit.

This backward glance at a two-thousand-year-old church tells us something important about the Spirit-filled life. It isn't always—or even often—flashy. It is *always* disciplined. And it is *always* a church at work.

Today, if your health allows, plan to skip one meal during the coming week. Ideally, do this with other Christians. This may mean skipping a meal at the same time and committing to prayer in separate places, or gathering virtually, or getting together in person. If your health doesn't allow it, devote that time, without fasting, to praying with others. And what should your prayer be? Simply, "What is the work you're calling us to?"

> *Holy Spirit,*
> *What is the work you're calling us to?*
> *And what is the work we're willing to do?*
> *Will we worship*
> *and serve*
> *and fast*
> *and pray*
> *To make room in our lives for your life-changing Word?*
> *Amen.*

19

Stay together

Don't you know that you yourselves are God's temple and that God's Spirit dwells in your midst? If anyone destroys God's temple, God will destroy that person; for God's temple is sacred, and you together are that temple.

—1 Corinthians 3:16–17 NIV

A marriage-counselor friend once told me, "It takes two to get married, but one to get divorced." Simply put, it's easier to break a relationship than to build one.

We've gotten used to a broken church. I grew up in a church that used catchphrases like "in essentials, unity; in opinions, liberty; in all things, love." Then we split over whether to use musical instruments in worship.

We may be used to division, but Paul wasn't. That's why in Greek he used plurals that aren't clear in English: *You* is *y'all*. *Y'all* are God's temple; God's Spirit dwells in *y'all*. (Remember the Hebrew on day 17? It's the same here in Greek.)

Paul was so committed to unity that he used tough language in today's passage to condemn division: "If anyone destroys God's temple, God will destroy that person."

This is Old Testament lawcourt language, which uses the pattern "if—then." *If* you do something wrong, *then* this is the penalty. Crime yields punishment. For instance, one Old Testament law reads, "If anyone uncovers a pit or digs one and fails to cover it and an ox or a donkey falls into it, the one who opened the pit must pay the owner for the loss and take the dead animal in exchange" (Exodus 21:33–34).

Paul took division-makers, church-dividers, to court, so to speak. Paul warned, if we destroy—divide—the church, we will be destroyed!

But how do we destroy the church?

Certain Corinthians had twisted the Spirit-filled life into a source of division. They argued over who was the best leader—Paul, Peter, Apollos or Christ. They argued over who was most spiritual, those who ate meat sacrificed to idols or those who didn't. They argued over who practiced the best spiritual gift, with speaking in tongues topping the chart.

Adept at arguing, they missed the secret of the Spirit-filled life, that unity is precious, that we—not just me—are together a Spirit-filled temple.

Reach out today to one person who belongs to a different Christian community from you, who holds a different point of view on hot topics, who worships differently from you. Bring to them a word of encouragement, of grace, of gratitude, because they, too, belong to the same Spirit-filled temple as you.

> *Holy Spirit,*
>> *Sometimes I want to divvy up the church*
>>> *since I'm partial to partitions*
>>>> *and disposed to divisions*
>> *Instead, let me build and bring together*
>>> *even a small corner of your Spirit-filled temple.*
>>>> *Amen.*

20

Struggle for harmony

Make every effort to keep the unity of the Spirit through
the bond of peace.

—Ephesians 4:3 NIV

Paul's prison language—he himself was "a prisoner for the
Lord" (Ephesians 4:1)—underscores the intensity of his
appeal for unity. As he looked around his Roman jail cell,
he fetched for words—and found them! The verb *keep*,
in "keep the unity of the Spirit," means to guard, like the
prison guards keeping Paul chained. The noun *bond*, in "the
bond of peace," means chains, fetters or shackles, which
held Paul in his prison cell.

This prison language tells us that unity doesn't come naturally. We need to drop cozy images of church—everyone getting along, gathering happily and living in sweet harmony. Paul knew better. He knew that unity will escape without alert guards.

But how? How to guard the unity of the Spirit? The answer lies in what Paul just said in the previous verse: "Be completely humble and gentle; be patient, bearing with one another in love" (Ephesians 4:2). *All* humility. (He adds, *completely—all* in Greek—because humility is often in short supply.) Gentleness. Patience. It's easier to be self-satisfied, harsh and impatient. These qualities come naturally. But they won't guard the unity of the Spirit in the fetters of peace.

There's another way, too, to guard the unity of the Spirit. We may be tempted to look at what divides us. Political opinions, variations in skin color, differences in doctrine, distinctions in worship styles. It's not hard to find what separates us. To guard the unity of the Spirit, we need to look hard at what *unites* us. So Paul continued in the next verses, "There is one body and one Spirit, just as you were called to one hope when you were called; one Lord, one faith, one baptism; one God and Father of all, who is over all and through all and in all" (Ephesians 4:4–6). That's seven *ones* in a row. Our church is one under one God. Shouldn't we live into this reality?

For the second day in a row, reach out to someone who doesn't share your doctrine, worship style, skin color or politics (or anything else that separates you from them). Talk with them about what unites you. Perhaps adopt Ephesians 4:4–6 as a guide. Discuss how, despite strong differences, you can still share one body, one Spirit, one hope, one Lord, one faith, one baptism and one God.

> *Holy Spirit,*
> > *when I see only differences*
> > *when my mind is made up*
> > *remind me—*
> > > *humility*
> > > *gentleness*
> > > *patience*
> > *are standing guard over the unity you inspire. Amen.*

21

Reflect on staying connected

I grew up in a small cookie-cutter home on Long Island. Our kitchen had a rectangular yellow Formica table with curved chrome legs. We ate every meal at that table. When my parents bought a round wooden table, that yellow Formica table became my junior high school desk.

Later, when I headed to graduate school, that yellow Formica table went with me. When Priscilla and I got married and eventually bought a house, that yellow Formica table took pride of place in our kitchen, which we painted yellow to match.

Then, when I was about forty, Priscilla and I had a fierce argument, which simmered and stewed and erupted like a volcano. Fifteen years in, our marriage was about to rupture. So we sat at that yellow Formica table, knee to knee, and argued—*argued fiercely*—long into the night, struggling to stay together.

And we did. Stay together, that is.

Staying together is such hard work. The authors of our Bible knew this. Ezekiel grasped that communities need a good Spirit-scrubbing—or the storm of Spirit-breath bringing dry bones back to life. Christians in Antioch strengthened community through disciplines. Paul challenged schism with the image of a Spirit-filled temple. And then, sitting in prison, he found just the right words for community—guard and bond, fetters and keep.

Today's photograph contains a symbol of community. Notice the bluebonnets, reflecting the beauty of people gathered around a table in harmony. Notice the candelabra, expressing the invitation to eat, laugh and join with friends and strangers for a feast. But ponder, too, the yellow Formica table itself, where Priscilla and I sat long into the night, and pause to consider the struggle required for communities, even Spirit-filled communities, to stay together.

This, then, is the third secret of the Spirit-filled life: *To commit to community, we need to "make every effort to keep the unity of the Spirit through the bond of peace"* (Ephesians 4:3 NIV).

As you take some time to reflect upon my yellow Formica table, find a symbol of your own that represents your commitment to staying together, whether in a friendship, a church or a marriage. Identify challenges that threaten to pull that relationship apart. Identify, as well, one practical strategy that will strengthen you to "make every effort to keep the unity of the Spirit through the bond of peace."

> *Holy Spirit,*
>> *You are the source of harmony, the spring of unity*
>>> *When I want to give up on others*
>>>> *and go it alone*
>>> *Remind me that I experience you*
>>>> *in the marvel of uncommon unity*
>>>> *in the miracle of hard-won harmony. Amen.*

FIND THE HEART
OF THE SPIRIT

*Discover the energy
of the Holy Spirit in you*

22

Breathe the breath of justice

> Thus says God the LORD,
> Who created the heavens and stretched them out,
> Who spread forth the earth and that which
>   comes from it,
> Who gives breath to the people on it,
> And spirit to those who walk on it.
>
> —Isaiah 42:5 NKJV

It's the start of week four, so we return, as we do every week, to the bedrock reality of the Spirit-filled life: Spirit is breath, breath is Spirit. It's back to basics again.

In Genesis, God breathed into a lump of lifeless clay, face-to-face, so that it "became a living being," Adam—in Hebrew, *human* (Genesis 2:7). In Genesis, God breathed in *n^eshamah*, but in Isaiah 42:5, God breathed in *n^eshamah* and *ruach*. Breath, in Isaiah's Hebrew poetry, is Spirit. Spirit and breath, in short, are one and the same.

In the Spirit-filled life, there can be no hiding behind false dichotomies, like sacred versus secular, physical versus spiritual. God's creation is God's creation. Period.

Isaiah knew, too, that creation was not a one-off event. God *is* the Creator. That's why Isaiah in Hebrew said that God gives—not *gave*—breath. God gives—not *gave*—Spirit to those who walk on this daily designed earth.

The New International Version gets today's passage right: "The Creator of the heavens, who stretches them out, who spreads out the earth" (Isaiah 42:5 NIV). See that? *Present tense.* God is ever the Creator.

But here's the rub. The gift of Spirit-breath in Isaiah 42:5 is wedged between stunning descriptions of a servant who will transform the world by establishing justice.

This is what the servant of God does:

- brings forth justice to the nations (42:1).
- brings forth justice for truth (42:3).
- opens blind eyes (42:7).
- brings out of prison those who sit in darkness (42:7).

God has big plans for God's servants. Plans brimming with justice. God's servants bring forth justice—the prophet says this *twice!*—to open blind eyes, rescue prisoners, shine light for those in darkness.

God gives us Spirit-breath, yes, and with Spirit-breath big responsibilities. That is why we have to take a big, deep breath and then get moving—to the corners of the earth, even dark prisons. To that end, God gives us—present tense—Spirit-breath.

───

Knowing that *ruach* is Spirit-breath, *God's* breath in you, breathe in and out deeply for four minutes at this, the start of week four. (Set a timer, if need be.) If you are able, take a four-minute walk, since Isaiah refers to those who *walk* on the earth. As you walk, breathe deeply and slowly, looking and listening intently for a role you can play—one small, practical step—to bring forth justice.

> Holy Spirit,
>> I panic in the darkness
>> Holding my breath for fear
>> Teach me to breathe again
>>> to walk this earth
>>>> with justice brimming
>>>> with truth teeming
>>>> with light shining. Amen.

23

Receive the Spirit of adoption

For you did not receive a spirit of slavery to fall back into fear, but you have received a spirit of adoption. When we cry, "Abba! Father!" it is that very Spirit bearing witness with our spirit that we are children of God.

—Romans 8:15–16 NRSV

Had you lived in Rome during Paul's day, you might have seen some people walking around with odd hats, some of them pointed and conical, even slightly comical and clown-like. These funny-looking hats were anything but funny. They were caps of manumission—caps freed slaves wore to demonstrate to everyone that they were now free. On some coffins of the wealthy, you still see carvings of men and women wearing these caps because slaves were often manumitted—freed—at the death of their owners.

This is the image Paul pressed into service to fire the imagination of Roman believers. We are like manumitted slaves, the whole of whose future is now open-ended.

But this was not enough for the apostle Paul. Christians are not just free. They are free to become part of a family. They are freed, yes, but adopted, too.

If slavery is hopeless labor and unrequited toil, with no circle of security, no intimacy, no embrace, then adoption, in contrast, extends the circle and care and kindness of a family. The Spirit-filled life takes place within that family circle, where the Spirit, deep within, inspires the prayer, "Abba! Father!"

These tandem realities—manumission and adoption—don't lead to a complicated web of relationships. They lead to one: *Abba! Father!*

The most suitable prayer in response to being freed and adopted, therefore, isn't complicated. Or theologically sophisticated. Or flowery. Freed and adopted, we pray simply, *Abba! Father!*

You're at the heart of the Spirit-filled life now, with the simplest of prayers, *Abba! Father!*, expressing the simplest of relationships: *We're children of God.* "When we cry, 'Abba! Father!' it is that very Spirit bearing witness with our spirit that we are children of God" (Romans 8:16). Or, as Romans 8:15 in *The Message* reads, we, as children of God, are "adventurously expectant, greeting God with a childlike 'What's next, Papa?'"

Today, our job is to accomplish nothing, to initiate nothing, to begin nothing new. Today, our job is to realize that *God* has manumitted us, *God* has initiated adoption proceedings. We can't even claim credit for prayer because the *Holy Spirit* prompts prayer within us! So take some time today to sit and breathe—and get back to the basics of the Spirit-filled life. As you breathe in, say simply the first part of this simple prayer, *Abba* or *What's next?* or some other prayer that addresses God intimately. And as you breathe out, say simply, *Father* or *Papa* or some other simple prayer that addresses God intimately. Whatever you say, however you pray, pray this prayer throughout your day today.

> *Holy Spirit,*
> *Inspire me to pray*
> *Rouse me to speak*
> *Not many words, just two*
> > *two words that matter most: Abba! Father! Amen.*

24

Confess the one truth
that matters

Now about the gifts of the Spirit, brothers and sisters, I do not want you to be uninformed. You know that when you were pagans, somehow or other you were influenced and led astray to mute idols. Therefore I want you to know that no one who is speaking by the Spirit of God says, "Jesus be cursed," and no one can say, "Jesus is Lord," except by the Holy Spirit.

—1 Corinthians 12:1–3 NIV

In the second half of 1 Corinthians, Paul answered questions penned in a letter the Corinthians had sent to him. He signaled answers with the Greek word *peri,* "concerning" or "for." The whole section, in fact, begins, "Now for [*peri*] the matters you wrote about" (7:1).

Paul began his answer to their question about spiritual gifts in the same way: "Now about [*peri*] the gifts of the Spirit, brothers and sisters, I do not want you to be uninformed" (12:1).

The problem is that he *did* leave them uninformed—at least about spiritual gifts! Paul didn't answer their question. Not right away, at least.

Instead, he took them back to basics. No one says "Jesus is cursed" by the Spirit of God, and no one says "Jesus is Lord" except by the Holy Spirit.

Why take them back to basics rather than answering their question? Because the Greek word the Corinthians used for spiritual gifts, *pneumatika*, was a prickly and flawed word. Some of the Corinthians claimed to be *pneumatikoi*—spiritual elite. They believed that their experience of the gifts of the Spirit somehow made them better than others.

Paul would have none of this.

They may have wanted to inhabit a hierarchical world based upon the perceived worth of various spiritual gifts, but Paul refused to play this game. He took them to another playing field altogether, back to basics, to the bedrock words "Jesus is Lord."

It's not spiritual gifts, important as they are, that matter most. What matters most is saying "Jesus is Lord."

We are all rooted in the same truth, the same words, the same belief. Every single Christian is united, not by a uniform experience of the Holy Spirit, but by the unifying confession "Jesus is Lord."

Yesterday, it was the simple prayer "Abba! Father!"

Today, it is the simple confession "Jesus is Lord."

These are the heartbeats of the Spirit-filled life.

If yesterday, you breathed in and out to the rhythm of *Abba! Father!,* today you will breathe in and out to the bedrock of faith: *Jesus is Lord.* As you breathe in, say simply, "Jesus." As you breathe out, say simply, "is Lord." If you wish, you can alternate "Abba! Father!" with "Jesus is Lord." Whatever you say and however you say it, live for a few minutes in the prayer and confession that unite all of us.

> *Holy Spirit,*
>> *if I am prone to prize my experience of you more than others'*
>> *if I am inclined to believe my gifts are more valuable than others'*
>> *if I am disposed to insist my spiritual life is more vital than others'*
>> *Forgive me*
>> *Set me again on the bedrock of the Spirit-filled life: Jesus is Lord. Amen.*

25

Grow in the grace of spiritual gifts

Now there are varieties of gifts, but the same Spirit; and there are varieties of services, but the same Lord; and there are varieties of activities, but it is the same God who activates all of them in everyone.

—1 Corinthians 12:4–6 NRSV

We saw yesterday how Paul wouldn't tolerate Christians who thought their spiritual gifts made them better than others. So he went back to basics: The Spirit inspires the words *Jesus is Lord*.

Paul also sidestepped the Corinthians' term for spiritual gifts, *pneumatika*, because they'd used it to create a spiritual pecking order.

Instead, he supplied three words of his own:

- *charisma*
- *diakonia*
- *energēma*

Each word can dramatically deepen our understanding of spiritual gifts.

Charisma. Paul chose the word *charisma*, which communicates more than particular gifts given to particular individuals. The word *charisma* evokes the word *charis*, grace—to remind us of the unearned grace that is available to everyone, not just a few especially gifted Christians.

Diakonia. The purpose of spiritual gifts is *diakonia*: practical service. This goal could hardly be more evident than when Paul urged the Corinthians to complete their "service," *diakonia*, a financial gift for the Jerusalem church (2 Corinthians 8:4; 9:1; 9:12). This Greek word tells us that spiritual gifts aren't meant for the well-being of the gifted. The criterion of how well a spiritual gift has been *received* is how well it is *used* to serve others—because a spiritual gift is *diakonia*.

Energēma. The core of *energēma* (*energy* in English) is sheer power. Paul liked to use this noun with the related verb *energein* (to work). So Paul told the Corinthians, "there are varieties of activities [*energēmatōn*], but it is the same God who activates [*energōn*] all of them in everyone."

These three words put spiritual gifts into their proper perspective, as evidence of:

- grace that erases hierarchy;
- practical service that benefits others;
- energy that ignites all gifts.

Three words. Three powerful words that rewrite spiritual gifts, which are not so much what we receive as what we give when we show others grace, serve them well and use our God-given energy for their benefit.

For two days you've had the opportunity to breathe in and out, as you've returned to the bedrock prayer and confession of the Spirit-filled life. Now it's time to act. Take a few minutes of quiet reflection to identify one activity that overflows with grace, is aimed at practical service and may require a surge of divine energy to accomplish. Once you have identified this single action, large or small, make a concrete plan to set it in motion.

> *Holy Spirit,*
>> *fill me with grace, the source of spiritual gifts*
>> *groom me for service, the goal of spiritual gifts*
>> *fill me with energy, the fuel of spiritual gifts. Amen.*

26

Meet one Spirit in many gifts

All these are activated by one and the same Spirit, who
allots to each one individually just as the Spirit chooses.

—1 Corinthians 12:11 NRSV

In high school, I created a list of spiritual gifts, hoping to
figure out what my spiritual gift was. Was mine healing?
Prophecy? To determine my gift (oh, please! Let me have
one!), we read 1 Corinthians 12:4–11. Friends told me mine
was the gift of encouragement.

Look closely in your Bible, and you'll see that this list
is a catalog: *to another, to another, to another*. So on and so
on. Why so bland? Because Paul, the nemesis of spiritual
hierarchy, didn't dare feature one gift over the other. He
refused to fuel a desire for spiritual pecking orders.

But the conclusion to this list is anything but bland. It's robust. Vibrant. Excessive, even.

The conclusion begins with words in this order in Greek: "All these things energize the one and the same Spirit, who allots to each and every one . . ." All that happens through a message of knowledge, a message of wisdom, faith, healings, miracles, prophecy, discernment of spirits, speaking in tongues and the interpretation of tongues—all of these energize and are energized by one and the same Spirit.

Paul's language bursts at the seams.

In today's passage, the Spirit is "the one and the same." Paul could have said simply, as he did before, "the same Spirit." But Paul emphasized that a single source—*one* and the same—is responsible for *all* these energy bursts.

The power of this Spirit energizes "each one individually." Paul could have said simply, "everyone." So this is robust, too. Not a solitary soul is bereft of the Spirit's energy.

Yes, Paul's language here is enthusiastic, fueled by the realization that *one and the same* Spirit gives gifts to *each and every one*. Difference, diversity, variety—these point not to distinct points of origin, but to a single, solitary, spectacular source: the Holy Spirit.

There is marvel, awe, here—amazement at the compressed energy that issues, not in a single burst of light, but in a surprisingly varied series of surges that bring all of life to light.

Today, identify someone who seems to exercise very different gifts from yours. If you are a visionary, find a bean counter. If you are a doer, find someone who prays endlessly. If you love to talk, find someone skilled in listening. Spend time together, maybe over a cup of tea or coffee or a meal or on a walk, trying to understand how someone so different from you can receive energy from the one and the same Spirit.

> *Holy Spirit,*
> > *when I see difference as a threat to harmony*
> > > *diversity as a rival to unity*
> > *let me celebrate the gifts of others*
> > > *gifts I do not own*
> > *until I grasp that one and the same Spirit gives*
> > *gifts to each and everyone. Amen.*

27

Cultivate the character of Christ

The fruit of the Spirit is love, joy, peace, patience, kindness, generosity, faithfulness, gentleness, and self-control. There is no law against such things.

—Galatians 5:22–23 NRSV

In June 2021, Priscilla and I became faculty-in-residence at Southern Methodist University, so we now live full-time in a campus dorm filled with nearly two hundred students. During student orientation, we walked the halls with a blue wagon filled with snacks and drinks—a welcome wagon of sorts for sweating, fretting parents and incoming, excited students.

Then the parents left.

And with them, rules that had restrained students for eighteen years! A bevy of eighteen-year-olds discovered newfound freedom.

Freedom is what Paul helped the Galatians negotiate. Their newfound freedom in Christ. It's not pretty in college, and it wasn't in Galatia either. Tucked into Galatians 5, you'll find warnings like this:

> You were running a good race. Who cut in on you to keep you from obeying the truth?
>
> —v. 7 NIV

> But do not use your freedom to indulge the flesh; rather, serve one another humbly in love.
>
> —v. 13 NIV

> If you bite and devour each other, watch out or you will be destroyed by each other.
>
> —v. 15 NIV

Paul wasn't naïve. He knew the exercise of freedom could lead either to the flesh or the Spirit.

He also knew that life in the flesh is a whole lot easier to slip into than life in the Spirit. "Hatred, discord, jealousy, fits of rage, selfish ambition, dissensions, factions and envy" (vv. 20–21 NIV) come naturally.

Cultivating the fruit of the Spirit, in contrast, takes time and tending. But pluck an orange off a tree and peel it, pick a ripe tomato off a vine and bite into it, and you'll know instantly the worth of steady growth.

What fruit exactly does the Spirit yield? "Affection for others, exuberance about life, serenity. We develop a willingness to stick with things, a sense of compassion in the heart, and a conviction that a basic holiness permeates things and people" (v. 22 MESSAGE).

Notice, Paul didn't say fruits—plural. The fruit—singular—of the Spirit is a cohesive life, a focused life, a singular life, in which these qualities coalesce in goodness, *pure goodness*, like the juice of a freshly squeezed orange.

Review one day from the past week when you may have acted according to the flesh, with "hatred, discord, jealousy, fits of rage, selfish ambition, dissensions, factions and envy." Ask yourself what that situation would have been like if you had exhibited the fruit of the Spirit instead. Write both scenarios down—what happened and what might have happened—and notice the difference between them. Pray and plan for a better response next time.

> *Holy Spirit,*
> *When I choke on the bitterness of the flesh*
> *jealousy*
> *anger*
> *ambition*
> *let me taste the sweet fruit of the Spirit*
> *affection*
> *exuberance*
> *serenity. Amen.*

28

Reflect on the heart of the Spirit

This week, we've drilled down to bedrock.

- The earliest Christian prayer, *Abba! Father!*
- The earliest Christian confession, *Jesus is Lord.*
- The realization, expressed so emphatically by Paul, that one and the same Spirit gives gifts to each and everyone. There's no pecking order here.
- The awareness that none of this is our doing. God has adopted us. The Holy Spirit prompts prayer and gives gifts. No credit is due us. Not a cent.

- The knowledge that spiritual gifts are gifts of grace, *charismata* intimately tied to the spring of faith: *charis*, grace.

Today's photograph of oranges on the tree takes us back to basics. Look for a few quiet moments at the dappled texture of the orange peel, the curves and curls of the leaves, the gnarly and twiggy branches, the sun and shade. This is where sweetness begins, where it is unprocessed, unpackaged, unshipped. This fruit is full of life, full of flavor, full of promise.

Standing here, gazing at these oranges, imagine yourself filled with sweet, pure juice. You can do this, live this Spirit-filled life, unspoiled by artificial ingredients, fresh and full of flavor, because, as we saw yesterday, God "brings gifts into our lives, much the same way that fruit appears in an orchard—things like affection for others, exuberance about life, serenity. We develop a willingness to stick with things, a sense of compassion in the heart, and a conviction that a basic holiness permeates things and people" (Galatians 5:22 MESSAGE). Yes, we can live this way!

This, then, is the fourth secret of the Spirit-filled life: *A regular return to the basics keeps us fresh and focused on what really matters—our basic belief, our simple prayer and our modest embrace of humility, compassion and grace.*

Life, including the Spirit-filled life, can become complicated. So go back to the beginning, back to basics. Make a plan to include the simplest prayer, *Abba! Father!*, and the earliest confession, *Jesus is Lord!*, in your daily schedule. Write it down. Set a timer to recall and recite these throughout your day. As you do, remind yourself that sometimes simplicity is best, like the simple and sweet flavor of a fresh orange picked right off the tree.

> *Holy Spirit,*
> > *when life becomes complicated*
> > > *complex*
> > > *cluttered*
> > *lead me beside quiet waters*
> > *restore my soul*
> > *take me back to the beginning*
> > > *the basics*
> > > *the bedrock*
> *Abba! Father!*
> *Jesus is Lord!*
> *One and the same Spirit giving gifts*
> > *to each and everyone. Amen.*

GO WHERE THE
GOING GETS TOUGH

*Discover the Holy Spirit
in the wilderness*

29

Breathe the breath of mortality

> Do not put your trust in princes, in human
> beings, who cannot save.
> When their spirit departs, they return to the
> ground; on that very day, their plans come to
> nothing.
>
> —Psalm 146:3–4 NIV

The goal of the Spirit-filled life isn't just immortality. It's also coming to grips with mortality. That's what makes Psalm 146 so important.

In this psalm, we see that even the powerful can't escape death. "When their spirit departs, they return to the ground."

This claim is rich with the language of creation and curse in Genesis.

- Rulers are called human beings—in Hebrew, "sons of *adam*" (Psalm 146:3). Like the first *Adam*, they come from the earth. No one is powerful enough to escape death. Adam didn't. The powerful won't. We won't, either.
- The words "they return to the ground" also sound like Genesis—this time what God said to Adam in Genesis 3:19: "until you return to the ground, since from it you were taken; for dust you are and to dust you will return." The Hebrew in the psalm actually says, "they return to *their* ground." Death is personal. Princes and presidents end up in their own little plot of ground. Nothing more.
- Even "spirit" in the psalm is reminiscent of Genesis 2:7, though the poet replaces the original breath of life (*nᵉshamah*) of Genesis 2:7 with spirit (*ruach*). Breath is Spirit. Spirit is life—until our last breath.

We return to this baseline each week. The Spirit-filled life isn't spectacular, a series of significant victories. The Spirit-filled life is intertwined with the life we lead each seemingly insignificant day—the Spirit-breath we breathe, the dirt we're made of.

But that's not the end of the story (or the psalm). Later, you'll find the sort of people God is keen to help—oppressed, hungry, prisoners, blind, bowed down, foreigners, orphans and widows (Psalm 146:7–9).

We may be seduced by the powerful, but let's remember they'll return to the earth when their Spirit-breath departs. The Spirit-filled life leads elsewhere, to the community of the bereft and bowed down. That's where the going gets tough—and the Spirit keeps going.

Knowing that *ruach* is Spirit-breath, *God's* breath in you, breathe in and out deeply for five minutes at this, the start of week five. (Set a timer if need be.) As you breathe deeply and slowly, be mindful of people who are oppressed, hungry, prisoners, blind, bowed down, foreigners, orphans or widows (Psalm 146:7–9). As the Spirit calls them to mind, write their names down. Then take one small, practical step toward one of them today in order to transform a seemingly ordinary day into an eternally significant one.

> *Holy Spirit,*
>> *Ashes to ashes, dust to dust, destined for my little plot*
>>> *of earth*
>> *but, for now anyway, inbreathed, inspired, invited*
>> *You've invited me, not to a banquet of the rich*
>>> *the powerful, the desirable*
>>> *but to a celebration of the bowed down*
>> *To that celebration, Holy Spirit,*
>>> *I accept your invitation. Amen.*

30

Don't be frightened of what lies ahead

"But now be strong, Zerubbabel," declares the LORD. "Be strong, Joshua son of Jozadak, the high priest. Be strong, all you people of the land," declares the LORD, "and work. For I am with you," declares the LORD Almighty. "This is what I covenanted with you when you came out of Egypt. And my Spirit remains among you. Do not fear."

—Haggai 2:4–5 NIV

Old Testament prophet Haggai's grandparents were violently deported from Jerusalem to Babylon fifty years earlier. In the meantime, the Persian Empire defeated Babylon, and Cyrus, Persia's ruler, encouraged those in exile to return to their homelands to rebuild cities Babylon had destroyed. Haggai led a delegation of men and women as they returned to their homeland, determined to rebuild Jerusalem and restore the temple to its former glory.

Born in exile in Babylon, Haggai had never laid eyes on Jerusalem. What he saw when he arrived was devastating. Jerusalem lay in shambles. The people who returned from Persia before him stopped rebuilding. Drought had ruined their crops.

Haggai did not skulk away. He went where the going gets tough.

Work! he told the people. Every last one of them. Governor. High priest. Farmers.

Then, as an exclamation point to the command, he spoke for God: "My Spirit remains among you. Do not fear!" Though it reads *remain* or *abide* in English translations, the Hebrew verb here is *stand*. My Spirit *stands* among you.

This particular verb, *stand*, recalls the exodus, when Israelite slaves escaped from Egypt. Pinned between the Egyptian army and the sea, they faced annihilation. Yet that night, as peril reared its ugly head, a miraculous pillar of cloud "moved from in front and stood behind them, coming between the armies of Egypt and Israel" (Exodus 14:19–20).

The pillar *stood* between the Israelites and the Egyptians, hot in pursuit, protecting them all night long.

Faced with the intimidating task of motivating workers demoralized by drought to rebuild the temple ruins, Haggai could have assumed God had abandoned them. He didn't. Haggai instead transformed the first exodus into *their* exodus: *My Spirit stands among you.* There was no pillar,

Haggai knew. But someone else was standing among them in a battered Jerusalem—the Spirit, *ruach,* stood now like the pillar on that first night of liberation, vigilant and sturdy, offering protection during tough days ahead.

———

Take three steps today to overcome this sense of anxiety and uncertainty. Begin by taking one minute to identify your most pressing anxieties. What makes you most anxious? Continue with two minutes more to imagine the Spirit standing in the middle of those anxieties, like the pillar that stood between the Egyptian army and the escaping slaves. Finally, take three more minutes to plan, as Haggai commanded, how to *work*! Plan one action, however small, to confront an anxiety that presses upon you. Remind yourself: *The Spirit stands right here.*

> *Holy Spirit,*
>   *I hesitate*
>   *paralyzed by anxiety*
>   *frozen by fear*
>   *Yet you stand in our midst*
>   *vigilant*
>   *alert*
>   *Let me see you standing there—standing here*
>   *And let me get to work rebuilding, refining,*
>   *reimagining my world. Amen.*

31

Head into the desert

It came to pass in those days that Jesus came from Nazareth of Galilee, and was baptized by John in the Jordan. And immediately, coming up from the water, He saw the heavens parting and the Spirit descending upon Him like a dove. Then a voice came from heaven, "You are My beloved Son, in whom I am well pleased." Immediately the Spirit drove Him into the wilderness.

—Mark 1:9–12 NKJV

Still wet to the touch from his baptism, Jesus looked up and saw a dove descending. This was Jesus' moment, his intimate experience of the Holy Spirit. Jesus even heard God say, "You are My beloved Son, in whom I am well pleased."

This is what being filled with the Spirit should look like: the perfect realization that we are God's beloved children. *Abba! Father!*

It should look this way—but it doesn't always. Not for Jesus, anyway.

The Spirit turned on a dime, hurling Jesus immediately into the desert. As soon as he had a moment of clarity, it was torn from him. The truest measure of clarity would emerge for Jesus, not in the Spirit-filling at the Jordan River, however idyllic that was, but in the days of testing to follow.

So the Spirit *drove him out*—*ekballein* in Greek, as in *ballistic* missile—in the same way that Jesus *drove out* demons (Mark 1:34, 39), *drove out* leprosy (1:42), *drove out* money changers from the temple (11:15). Jesus urged, "If your eye causes you to stumble, *drive it out*" (9:47, my translation). The gentleness of a dove gave way to the violent force of the Spirit.

It's tempting to see spells in the desert, periods of spiritual drought, interludes without the enthralling exercise of spiritual gifts, as times of emptiness, of desolation. The story of Jesus tells us otherwise. The Holy Spirit could easily have kept Jesus along the grassy shore of the Jordan River, in earshot of words like "beloved" and "My Son." But the Spirit didn't let him linger in those pleasant confines, with heaven opened, a divine voice whispering words of love, a dove's docile descent.

The Spirit instead sent Jesus to a place he otherwise would never have gone, where his very existence was at risk. There, in the desert, God's provision was put to the test—and proven to be true.

························

Take a few moments today to identify a situation you would describe as a desert. Ask yourself, *If the Spirit drove Jesus into the desert to learn what he couldn't on the peaceful shore of the Jordan River, what will I learn if the Spirit drives me into the desert for a time?* Then, as you have the strength, take one practical step today to prepare to enter that desert, where the going gets tough.

> *Holy Spirit,*
>> *I hunger for your fruit—love, joy and peace*
>> *But for the food of the desert?*
>>> *Locusts. Honey.*
>>> *Desolation. Isolation. Separation.*
>> *No. Thank you.*
>>> *Into the desert you'll need to drive me—*
>>>> *like demons, leprosy, and money changers*
>>>> *like an errant eye plucked out, driven away.*
>> *If you do—when you do—drive me there, help me to say*
>> *Yes. Thank you. Amen.*

32

Follow your guide in the desert

Jesus, full of the Holy Spirit, returned from the Jordan and was led by the Spirit in the wilderness, where for forty days he was tempted by the devil.

—Luke 4:1–2 NRSV

In Mark's gospel, we just saw, the Spirit *drove* Jesus *out* into the desert.

Whew! Mark left us reeling—will the Spirit drive *us* into the desert?—but Luke is gentler. The Holy Spirit did not toss Jesus out. The Spirit escorted Jesus, guiding, leading, accompanying him through the desert.

The Greek verb translated as *led* in today's passage is bland. The scene itself is anything but. Jesus came out of the Jordan River, the Spirit descended upon him, and that same Spirit led him into the wilderness for forty days.

If you know your Old Testament, this will sound familiar. The Israelites emerged from the Red Sea, where an angel, along with pillars of cloud and fire, *led* them in the wilderness for forty years.

Israel's story must have been on Jesus' mind in the desert. Three times while he was tested, Jesus rejected Satan's advances by quoting from the book of Deuteronomy (8:3; 6:13; and 6:16), which features how God "led you [Israel] for forty years in the wilderness. The clothes on your back have not worn out, and the sandals on your feet have not worn out" (Deuteronomy 29:5).

So what do we learn for ourselves from how the Spirit led Jesus in the wilderness?

We learn again the second secret of the Spirit-filled life: The study of Scripture is vital for a robust Spirit-filled life. Jesus, led by the Spirit in the desert, quoted from the Old Testament when he was confronted by a cunning opponent. Jesus, Spirit-filled, knew his Bible by heart.

Just as indispensable, but maybe tougher to stomach, Jesus' Spirit-filled life was chock-full of hostility. The desert. The devil. The drama of temptation. The Spirit did not—this is the key—deliver Jesus from testing. The Spirit might have led him, as the pillars and angel led Israel through the desert, but the Spirit never rescued Jesus from that fitful, fateful, forty-day test.

Yesterday, you were asked to take a few moments to identify a situation you would describe as a desert—and take one practical step toward that desert. Today, your application may be harder. Take a few minutes to identify how you might be *guided by the Spirit* in that desert. After reading the first thirty-two reflections in this book, try to answer these questions: How can you prepare for that leading in the desert? What will such leading look like? What will be the goal of the Spirit's leading?

> *Holy Spirit,*
>> *When I am put to the test*
>> *When you put me in a place to take the test*
>> *Train my mind to recognize I need this test*
>> *Train my heart to believe I can face this test*
>> *Train my eye to see you there*
>>> *guiding me through that test. Amen.*

33

Seek the Spirit in a world of snakes and scorpions

Which of you fathers, if your son asks for a fish, will give him a snake instead? Or if he asks for an egg, will give him a scorpion? If you then, though you are evil, know how to give good gifts to your children, how much more will your Father in heaven give the Holy Spirit to those who ask him!

—Luke 11:11–13 NIV

Jesus prayed. Overwhelmed by crowds in need of healing, he prayed (Luke 5:16). Facing decisions, such as who should be his disciples, he prayed (Luke 6:12). In anguish facing death, he prayed (Luke 22:44).

Seeing this, Jesus' disciples demanded, "Lord, teach us to pray" (Luke 11:1). So he did, starting with the content of prayer: "Our Father which art in heaven, hallowed be thy name" (Matthew 6:9 KJV).

Yet Jesus taught them not just *what* to pray, but *how* to pray. He encouraged them to be tenacious in prayer: "Everyone who asks receives; the one who seeks finds; and to the one who knocks, the door will be opened" (Luke 11:10).

Then Jesus said something really strange—about snakes and scorpions. Why bring up scorpions and snakes in a promise about the Holy Spirit?

Because Jesus had faced evil head-on. He knew that the Spirit-filled life is never far from a world writhing with snakes and teeming with scorpions.

Remember how the Spirit led Jesus in the desert for forty days (Luke 4:1–2)? The backdrop of that story is Israel's wandering in the desert for forty years after their exodus from Egypt. Moses told them to remember "the LORD your God, who brought you out of Egypt, out of the land of slavery" and "led you through the vast and dreadful wilderness, that thirsty and waterless land, with its venomous snakes and scorpions" (Deuteronomy 8:14–15).

Jesus knew. He'd been there, where Israel had gone before. Jesus promised that God would not give praying people snakes and scorpions because God had led Israel—had led *him*—in a desert at the start, where he wrestled with evil.

And Jesus calls us now to wrestle with evil. For that kind of prayer, we need the Holy Spirit. However dark, however dire our hope, however agonizing our face-off with evil, we can experience the Holy Spirit, even in a desert teeming with snakes and scorpions, where the going gets tough.

God is the *Giver* of the Spirit, so put yourself in a position to *receive* the Spirit. If possible, set aside at least thirty minutes in the next few days to pray simply for openness to the Holy Spirit—by listening, reading Scripture, singing, breathing deeply—whatever opens you to the Spirit, who leads you through the desert, with its scorpions and snakes.

> *Holy Spirit,*
> > *I want to pray, "Make me lie down in green pastures"*
> > > *and "Lead me beside quiet waters"*
> > *I need to pray, "Prepare a table before me in the*
> > > *presence of my enemies"*
> > *Because*
> > > *there is bald-faced evil out there, where you want to*
> > > > *lead me—snakes and scorpions*
> > > *and secret evil in here, in me, where you want to*
> > > > *live—scorpions and snakes*
> > *Wherever evil is, outside or in, in others or in me*
> > > *lead me there and let me live. Amen.*

34

Stand faithful and speak faithfully

You must be on your guard. You will be handed over to the local councils and flogged in the synagogues. On account of me you will stand before governors and kings as witnesses to them. And the gospel must first be preached to all nations. Whenever you are arrested and brought to trial, do not worry beforehand about what to say. Just say whatever is given you at the time, for it is not you speaking, but the Holy Spirit.

—Mark 13:9–11 NIV

Spirit-filled Christians go where the going gets tough, and it doesn't get any tougher than here, where Jesus promises the Holy Spirit to people who are handed over, against their will, to official government persecution. Then, and only then, promises Jesus, will the Holy Spirit speak through them.

This is such an important promise that it features in three gospels. In each of them, the promise is given to those on the brink of martyrdom. Jesus promises each time:

> On my account you will be brought before governors and kings as witnesses to them and to the Gentiles. But when they arrest you, do not worry about what to say or how to say it. At that time you will be given what to say, for it will not be you speaking, but the Spirit of your Father speaking through you.
>
> —Matthew 10:18–20

> Whenever you are arrested and brought to trial, do not worry beforehand about what to say. Just say whatever is given you at the time, for it is not you speaking, but the Holy Spirit.
>
> —Mark 13:11

> When you are brought before synagogues, rulers and authorities, do not worry about how you will defend yourselves or what you will say, for the Holy Spirit will teach you at that time what you should say.
>
> —Luke 12:11–12

This promise is aimed at faithful followers whose backs are against the wall of official persecution, who haven't got time to prepare a defense because they've been taken forcibly from their homes and made to stand trial. It's not meant for those of us who have the opportunity to study, think, consider, plan, ponder and contemplate.

Even for those whose backs are against the wall, Jesus doesn't promise escape. He promises faithful witness—in Greek, *martyrion*—like the English word *martyr*. When the going gets tough, the Spirit is there, Jesus promises, not with a miraculous rescue but with a word of faithful witness.

———

Although you may not be persecuted by government officials, you can support those who are. Pray today for Christians who are being persecuted. If you aren't aware of any, take a few moments to find out about some. If you can't identify someone currently being persecuted for faith, look for past examples of faithful Christian martyrs—there are a good many—and express your gratitude for them, praying, too, that you would be open to a word of the Holy Spirit if your back were against the wall.

> *Holy Spirit,*
>> *Safety and success*
>>> *these are what I crave*
>> *Rejection and refusal*
>>> *these cause me to cave*
>> *Sharpen me for*
>>> *witness*
>>> *endurance*
>>> *truth*
>> *So that I can hear you when you speak*
>> *And bear it when you bear witness to the truth. Amen.*

35

Reflect on courage in the desert

A canal runs near the campus where I taught in Seattle. I'd walk along that canal and watch the salmon swim upstream to spawn. They're scarred, with scales missing, hook marks and bites etched on their bodies. *And they're still swimming.* These are the salmon that survive, the ones that make it, the hope of the future.

I'd tell my students that I teach for when they're forty, when they're black and blue. I'm honest about doubt, frank about faith. I'm still believing, still swimming—if upstream.

That, in a nutshell, is the point of this week. The Holy Spirit is alert and active, not just when the going is good, but when the going gets tough.

* Standing like a pillar as we face overwhelming challenges.

- Driving us into the desert.
- Leading us through the wilderness.
- Meeting us with a word of gospel truth when our backs are against the wall.

Today's photograph expresses this dimension of the Spirit-filled life. Pretend you're standing on the edge of this photograph and reflect for a moment on how you'll enter the scene. Notice the harsh desert growth underfoot, hugging the ground. Spot the path that leads nowhere or, worse yet, to the slopes of an unforgiving mountain. See the wrinkles on the mountainside; ask yourself whether you'll walk the ridges or the valleys. Consider even the ominous clouds, which hold little promise of rain but ample menace.

As you stand at the edge of this scene, imagine how you'd experience the Holy Spirit there. Not in the pleasant confines of a church or coffee shop or cozy couch—but in the desert, as you walk along desolate paths, perilous ridges and bleak valleys. Imagine the Holy Spirit *there*!

This, then, is the fifth secret of the Spirit-filled life: *The Holy Spirit accompanies us in the desert we inevitably face, and like a pillar in the darkest of nights, stands watch, along the edge of despair and hope.*

At the start of it all, after his baptism in the Jordan River, Jesus received the Spirit and heard the words, "You are My Son, whom I love; with you I am well pleased." With these words, God braced

Jesus for the forty days he would soon spend in the desert. Today, as you reflect on this photograph, consider whether you have what it takes to endure the desert. If you think you're ready, write down what has prepared you for the dangers that lie ahead. If you *don't* think you're ready—or if you find yourself in the desert right now—page back through the first five weeks of this book, looking for one—just one—reflection that especially speaks to you, and one—just one—application you can do, or do again, to sustain you as you confront the challenges of the desert.

> *Holy Spirit,*
> *I think to myself*
> *I'm just a son of Adam, a daughter of Eve*
> *Dust and dirt and destined for death*
> *And then*
> *I watch the salmon—scarred but single-minded*
> *I see the survivors—blemished but relentless*
> *So I pray*
> *Drive me to the desert*
> *Lead me in the wilderness*
> *Teach me*
> *To swim upstream*
> *until I'm home again*
> *To cherish the wasteland*
> *until I've learned what endures*
> *To have a faithful word on my lips*
> *at the end of the day. Amen.*

BREAK OUT OF THE FAMILIAR

Discover how the
Holy Spirit transforms our world

36

Breathe the breath of courage

But me—I'm filled with GOD's power, filled with GOD's Spirit of justice and strength, ready to confront Jacob's crime and Israel's sin.

—Micah 3:8 MESSAGE

Micah was a small-town prophet. (He's famous for his Christmas prediction that a ruler would come out of small-town Bethlehem rather than big-city Jerusalem.) He could have had a good, small life in a safe, small town. He could have lived his whole life in the comfort of the familiar.

He didn't. Not Micah.

Instead, he lambasted his fellow prophets: "The preachers who lie to my people. For as long as they're well paid and well fed, the prophets preach, 'Isn't life wonderful! Peace to all!' But if you don't pay up and jump on their bandwagon, their 'God bless you' turns into 'God damn you'" (Micah 3:5). With that, Micah forfeited the familiar fellowship of prophets.

But he had more to say: "The sun has set on the prophets. They've had their day; from now on it's night. Visionaries will be confused" (Micah 3:6–7). Prophets in Micah's day claimed to know the truth through visions, but Micah would have none of this.

The Spirit, he knew, is tied not to seeing visions but to seeing injustice. That's why he says, "But me—I'm filled with GOD's power, filled with GOD's Spirit of justice and strength, ready to confront Jacob's crime and Israel's sin" (Micah 3:8).

Micah knew that visions mean nothing when they are rooted in a thirst for comfort and convenience, the sort of comfort that avoids hard truths, the sort of convenience that says, "Isn't life wonderful! Peace to all!" as long as "they're well paid and well fed."

That's what his fellow prophets did. They made the Spirit-filled life captive to comfort.

Not Micah, who believed that the heart of the Spirit-filled life is not the occasional vision, the remarkable revelation, but the constant courage to challenge injustice.

If his fellow prophets gasped with visions and gaped at revelations, Micah was stuck with a call to call out injustice. Which, Spirit-filled as he was, is exactly what Micah did.

························

Knowing that *ruach* is Spirit-breath, *God's* breath in you, breathe in and out deeply for six minutes at this, the start of week six. (Set a timer, if need be.) As you breathe in, deeply and slowly, become aware of ways in which you set up your life this past week to keep yourself safe and secure. As you breathe out, slowly and deeply, become aware of ways in which you can, like Micah, break out of the familiar this coming week.

> *Holy Spirit,*
> > *As long as I'm well fed and well paid*
> > > *I'm all in*
> > *As long as I'm with friendly people in familiar*
> > > *surroundings*
> > > *I'm all yours*
> > *Am I?*
> > *Give me the courage this week*
> > > *to break out of the familiar*
> > > *to meet you in the unfamiliar*
> > *And still be all in, all yours, always. Amen.*

37

Find the Spirit among the unexpected

And it shall come to pass afterward that I will pour out My Spirit on all flesh; your sons and your daughters shall prophesy, your old men shall dream dreams, your young men shall see visions. And also on My menservants and on My maidservants I will pour out My Spirit in those days.

—Joel 2:28–29 NKJV

The book of Joel is pretty ordinary. There's no prophet wedded to a prostitute, like in Hosea. No vision of God whose robe fills the temple, like in Isaiah. No chariot with four-headed beasts, like in the book of Ezekiel.

No. Joel is pretty normal, as far as prophetic books go.

Except for this promise, which changes everything. I mean *everything*—how we value every person, every community, every nation.

Because *all* flesh isn't *some* flesh. Privileged flesh. Partial flesh. Particular flesh.

All flesh in the Bible includes animals, believe it or not (Genesis 6:19), and every sort of person the world over (Genesis 6:12; Deuteronomy 5:26; Psalm 65:2; Isaiah 49:26; 66:23).

All flesh means what it says: *all* flesh.

No single nation, no solitary continent, no select race receives the Spirit.

What's so amazing about this promise? It gives us an inside view of God. It's open-heart surgery on God.

God doesn't see a map with borders—towns, counties, states, nations.

I will pour out My Spirit on all flesh. Boundless, borderless, limitless, endless outpouring.

God doesn't privilege anyone—the gifted, the brilliant, the healthy, the wealthy.

I will pour out My Spirit on all flesh. Sons and daughters, old and young men, slaves and maids.

God doesn't favor powerful people over trapped and trafficked women and men.

I will pour out My Spirit on all flesh. Menservants and maidservants, both. The Spirit is poured out on them, too. Male and female slaves.

When Jesus' friend Peter, centuries later, quoted this passage to explain the outpouring of the Holy Spirit during the feast of Pentecost, he added a few words that aren't in Joel's original promise: "And on My menservants and on My maidservants I will pour out My Spirit in those days; and they shall prophesy" (Acts 2:18).

And they shall prophesy. My menservants and My maidservants. *Prophets.*

Yes, the Spirit is poured out on them, too. *Especially* them.

Locate a map of the world. Turn it upside down. Reflect on what you see that gives you a glimpse of how God sees the world. Look at countries that are familiar and those that are unfamiliar. Each time you look at a different country, recite this promise from the book of Joel, *I will pour out My Spirit on all flesh*, emphasizing the word *all*.

> *Holy Spirit,*
> *Not dribbles or drops or drips*
> *I want more*
> *Drenching and dousing and drowning in you*
> *I pray for an outpour*
> *And courage*
> *Courage to meet all flesh—not just my friends*
> *to prize all flesh—not just my church*
> *to love all flesh—not just my country*
> *Courage to celebrate when you rain on all flesh*
> *when you reign over all flesh. Amen.*

38

Bring justice to the nations

Here is my servant, whom I uphold, my chosen, in whom
my soul delights; I have put my spirit upon him; he will
bring forth justice to the nations.

—Isaiah 42:1 NRSV

Beautiful description of the Spirit-filled Christian, isn't it?
Servant. Chosen. God's delight, even.

But what if, under the surface, something else is brewing? The Hebrew word for delight, *raṣah,* is often used in
the Old Testament of God's delight—or not—in offerings
and sacrifices.

Think of what God said through the eighth-century Old
Testament prophet Amos: "I hate, I despise your festivals,

and I take no delight in your solemn assemblies. Even though you offer me your burnt offerings and grain offerings, I will not accept them" (Amos 5:21–22).

What if, in Isaiah 42:1, God isn't saying, "I'm delighted by My servant?" but "I'm delighted by the *sacrifice* My servant is willing to make?"

This explains the next lines: "He will not cry or lift up his voice" (42:2). Throughout the book of Isaiah, crying expresses anguish (19:20; 33:7; 46:7; 65:14). The servant won't cry out in anguish.

Then, the servant "will not grow faint or be crushed" (42:4)

What's going on, that the servant should risk this sacrifice?

What's going on? He's breaking out of the familiar. Spirit-filled, he'll "bring forth justice to the nations" (42:1), establish justice on the earth (42:4), be "a light to the nations" (42:6). Even "the coastlands wait for his teaching" (42:4). Teaching— *Torah* in Hebrew—belongs to distant lands far beyond the borders of his own.

What a spectacular vision of justice for all—not just some. Light for all nations—not just one. Teaching for anyone—not just the chosen.

We don't know who this servant was exactly in Isaiah's day. Was he a prophet? A ruler? A faithful remnant in Israel? Whoever he was, his unfamiliar vision proved too much for some, pitting the servant against those who refused to believe that God cherished the nations as much as God cherished *their* nation. So they sabotaged him (50:6; 52:13–53:12).

Still, the servant, Spirit-filled to the end, wouldn't cry out or grow weak until he "established justice in the earth" (42:4).

Remember how yesterday we practiced seeing the world as God sees it, without borders, minus boundaries? Today, let's go a step further to break out of the familiar by experiencing the Spirit in the company of unfamiliar people. Go out of your way, even with a small gesture, to bring light, justice and learning—Torah—to someone outside your familiar circle of friends and family.

> *Holy Spirit,*
>> *Plant kernels of kindness in the furrows of my nation*
>> *Grow seeds of grace in the fields of my native land*
>> *But do even more than this with me, Holy Spirit*
>>> *No matter the cost, regardless the risk*
>> *Use me to bring justice to the nations*
>> *Inspire me to bring hope to their yearning*
>>> *truth to their learning*
>>> *aid in their returning to you. Amen.*

39

Lavish blessings on the poor

The Spirit of GOD, the Master, is on me
  because GOD anointed me.
He sent me to preach good news to the poor,
  heal the heartbroken,
Announce freedom to all captives,
  pardon all prisoners.

—Isaiah 61:1 MESSAGE

We know from this snippet of the Bible what the Holy Spirit prompts us to do: bring good news to the poor, bind up the heartbroken, proclaim freedom to captives and release men and women in prison who are too poor to pay off their debts. There is no sense trying to spiritualize this. These are economically poor, truly brokenhearted, actual captives, real prisoners. We are to bear good news, heal, announce and pardon. No small feat. This is enough, isn't it?

Not quite. Not for the Spirit-filled life, at least. In the next few verses, God gives surprising, even lavish, gifts to the poor. Those of us anointed with the Spirit are expected to "care for the needs of all who mourn in Zion, give them bouquets of roses instead of ashes, messages of joy instead of news of doom, a praising heart instead of a languid spirit" (Isaiah 61:3).

I once had a student who worked in a shelter for abused women. One day, she told me, she spent the whole day giving the women manicures, pedicures, facials and hair-cuts. Afterward, she dressed them in beautiful clothes and doused them in fragrant perfumes. At the end of the day, the women gathered together in a candlelit room in a local Presbyterian church, where they sat among rose petals and ate a lavish meal.

These women, for the rest of their lives, will remember the day when exotic oils were rubbed over their ne-glected—and abused—bodies, when they donned lovely clothes, when they whiled away the evening enjoying a feast, when they, for a single day at least, had their spirits lifted and their poverty erased. This young student who made this vision real modeled the Spirit-filled life when she—in the language of Isaiah—gave "them bouquets of roses instead of ashes, messages of joy instead of news of doom, a praising heart instead of a languid spirit."

Choose one action today you can do for someone in need. Make it lavish, unexpected, even outlandish—a gift flowing from extreme, Spirit-filled generosity.

> Holy Spirit,
>> Make me generous, genuinely generous
>> Outspoken with good news
>> Outrageous with good gifts
>> Outlandish with good grace. Amen.

40

Follow the Spirit to strangers

The Spirit told Philip, "Go to that chariot and stay near it." Then Philip ran up to the chariot and heard the man reading Isaiah the prophet. "Do you understand what you are reading?" Philip asked. "How can I," he said, "unless someone explains it to me?" So he invited Philip to come up and sit with him.

—Acts 8:29–31 NIV

The story of Philip, a leader in the earliest church, captures the essence of the Spirit-filled life. No need for flourishes. It's all right here.

The story begins in Samaria with breathtaking success. "When the crowds heard Philip and saw the signs he performed, they all paid close attention to what he said" (Acts 8:6). Even Simon, a magician called Great Power of God, "followed Philip everywhere, astonished by the great signs and miracles he saw" (8:13). Small wonder that "there was great joy in that city" (8:8).

Who wouldn't want Philip to shepherd such a revival? Apparently, God.

God told Philip to get up and go, so Philip got up and went (8:26–27), leaving behind a thriving community—a whole city living in joy. He went, get this, to a wilderness road. God can lead us from activity, even good activities, to the desert, where there is no noise, no racket, no success, even.

Just the Spirit.

In the desert, the Spirit said, *Go!* and Philip *ran*. He didn't drag his feet. Or amble. Or saunter. Eager, Philip *ran* toward a chariot.

Then Philip asked the stranger a simple question: "Do you understand what you are reading?"

Philip then joined the stranger in the chariot. He went up to the Ethiopian rather than making the Ethiopian come to him.

The Spirit-filled life is as simple as it is hard.

We leave the trappings of success to travel deserted roads.
We run—eager to meet strangers.
We turn those strangers into friends with simple questions.
We join them where they are comfortable and where we, perhaps, are not.

Picture today's passage. A black man and a (somewhat) white man. An Ethiopian and an Israelite. Picture them together, bouncing along in a chariot on a desolate road, stooped together over a scroll of Isaiah draped over their knees. It's a sight to behold—a sighting of the Spirit-filled life.

In order to break out of the familiar, approach one stranger or near-stranger with a question that demonstrates your interest in them. Keep the question simple, like Philip's. It may be about the coffee they are drinking or the book they are carrying or the mood they are in. Whatever it is, have some questions in your back pocket because the Spirit is on the move, and you want to be on the move—remember, Philip *ran*—to complete strangers, too.

Holy Spirit,
I am no Philip
  Ready to leave success behind
  Eager to meet strangers
  Quick with a simple question
  At home away from home
No. I am no Philip
  I am busy, worried, sometimes bone-weary
    certainly not keen to meet strangers
So inspire me, Holy Spirit
  to find strangers right here, right now
  to make them my friends
    with an eager stride
    through a simple question
    by stepping into their world
And I—no, you—will transform our world
  and me in the process
  one stranger at a time. Amen.

41

Discover the Spirit in difference

Now in the church that was at Antioch there were certain prophets and teachers: Barnabas, Simeon who was called Niger, Lucius of Cyrene, Manaen who had been brought up with Herod the tetrarch, and Saul. As they ministered to the Lord and fasted, the Holy Spirit said, "Now separate to Me Barnabas and Saul for the work to which I have called them."

—Acts 13:1–2 NKJV

You'd think Christian mission began in Jerusalem. Or Rome. Or Athens. It didn't. Mission began in Antioch, a coastal city in Syria, when the Holy Spirit gave the word to send out Barnabas and Saul, leaders from Jerusalem who'd taught in Antioch for a year.

Why Antioch?

For starters, the Holy Spirit asked them to do what they were already doing—be open to outsiders. After a persecution in Jerusalem, Jesus' followers were scattered hither and yon. Most were "preaching the word to no one but the Jews only." But some, "when they had come to Antioch, spoke to the Hellenists, preaching the Lord Jesus" (Acts 11:19–20). The Hellenists probably spoke Greek and might not have been Jewish. The point? Some people broke down barriers, even as refugees during a persecution, by speaking with people different from themselves. These intrepid souls settled in Antioch.

Another reason why mission began in Antioch is this: What the Holy Spirit asked them to do was a natural extension of who they already were—mission in a nutshell. Barnabas hailed from the Mediterranean island of Cyprus. Simeon, "who was called Niger," was from northern Africa. Lucius was from modern-day Libya—also Africa. Manaen came from Israel, since he was a friend of Herod Antipas, ruler in Israel. Saul—Paul—came from Tarsus in modern-day Turkey. What does this tell us? The leadership team in Antioch created a half-moon around the Mediterranean Sea, from Saul of Tarsus to Simeon and Lucius in northern Africa.

In today's passage, the church in Antioch was perfectly primed to receive a word from the Holy Spirit that would send Barnabas and Saul to crisscross the Mediterranean

Sea. How so? They'd already opened themselves to people different from themselves, and they were already a patchwork of people from across the Mediterranean.

Simply put, mission was a natural extension of what they were already doing and who they already were. And that is why the Holy Spirit launched Christian mission from Antioch.

———————

In chapter eighteen, we reflected on the disciplines that made the community in Antioch receptive to a word of the Holy Spirit: fasting, worship (or service) and prayer—lots of prayer. Today we are reflecting on the character of this community, how the Holy Spirit spoke a word of mission to them because they were already a global mission in a nutshell. Spend some moments now comparing the disciplines and character of your community with those of Antioch. Make a list of differences you notice. Then dream some aspirations—ways in which your community can become more like Antioch—and, in the spirit of Antioch, pray!

> *Holy Spirit,*
>> *Speak to me, but not to me alone*
>> *Speak to us, all of us*
>>> *about how to be open*
>>> *about how to be warm*
>>> *about how to be daring*
>> *A haven for people different from ourselves. Amen.*

42

Reflect on the risk of reaching out

One of my favorite class sessions ends with the parable of the Good Samaritan, from Luke 10:25–37. It's not a math class, but still, I ask students to count the verbs.

A priest went, saw and passed by a beaten man. That's three verbs in the Greek.

A Levite went, saw and passed by. Three again.

A Samaritan went, saw and had compassion. Still three (in Greek, at least)—though *passed by* becomes *had compassion*.

For many of us, that's enough. The cramp of compassion, pang of pity, sting of sympathy—this is enough to separate us from the callous priest and coldhearted Levite.

But the Samaritan didn't stop with compassion. He

* went to him
* bandaged his wounds

- poured oil and wine on them
- set him on his animal
- brought him to an inn and
- took care of him

At the inn, he
- took out two denarii
- gave them to the innkeeper and
- said, "Look after him, and when I return, I will re-imburse you for any extra expense you may have."

Count the verbs. Any one would be generous. Any *one*. But the calculus of this man was lavish—not calculated. He did, not *any* of them, but *all* of them.

The Spirit we've met this week, like this man, is outland-ish, outrageous, outgoing, outsized. A downpour. Victory garlands. Running up to strangers. Fasting and praying with people from other nations.

Today's photograph offers a similarly boundless pan-orama. Follow the road. Pause in the valley. In the forest. Up the mountainside. In the summer snow. And finally, glide in the billowy clouds that float above the horizon. Ask yourself, What am I willing to risk, where will I venture, to experience renewal, purpose and joy, as I partner with the Holy Spirit?

This, then, is the sixth secret of the Spirit-filled life: *Risks—not calculated risks, carefully gauged and guaranteed to succeed, but risks that reach beyond the familiar—take us to where the Holy Spirit is already hard at work.*

Ask yourself today where in the list of the Good Samaritan's verbs you'd be likely to stop. As you reflect, be honest with yourself. Once you've identified the last verb in the list you'd be comfortable doing, look at the next verb. (For instance, if you think you'd have compassion, then ask yourself how you'd actually go to the person who is hurt in some way, just as the Good Samaritan had compassion and actually went over to the beaten man.) Whatever the next verb is in the list, try to do something like it by creating a strategy, a plan, to go one verb further. In this way, you can break out of the familiar and discover how the Holy Spirit can transform our world—*through you!*

> *Holy Spirit,*
> *If I'm honest,*
> *I'm not sure I want to break out of the familiar*
> *to be out in a rainstorm*
> *to buy victory garlands for the poor*
> *to run right up to strangers*
>
> *If I'm honest*
> *I'm sure I want to stay in the familiar*
> *in a warm home*
> *in a comfortable community*
> *in the company of friends*
>
> *You have work to do, Holy Spirit*
> *Not just to transform the world out there*
> *But to transform the world within me*
> *Begin now. With me. Please. Amen.*

LEAVE A SPIRITUAL LEGACY

*Discover how to help others
experience the Holy Spirit*

43

Breathe the breath of intimacy

Then he took a deep breath and breathed into them. "Receive the Holy Spirit," he said. "If you forgive someone's sins, they're gone for good. If you don't forgive sins, what are you going to do with them?"

—John 20:22–23 MESSAGE

Translations tell us what Jesus did after his resurrection: He breathed on his beleaguered friends. The *King James Version, New International Version, New Revised Standard Version, English Standard Version* and *Common English Bible* all translate the Greek verb *emphysaō* as breathed *on*.

But that's not quite accurate. *The Message*, on the other hand, gets it right: "Then he took a deep breath and breathed into them." *Into*. Not *on*.

There's a world of difference.

Breathing *on* is something we do with our glasses before cleaning them with a rag. Breathing *in* is something more—a startling closeness—like mouth-to-mouth resuscitation. Or, better yet, a kiss.

This verb, *emphysaō*, occurs first in the Greek Old Testament—the Bible the first Christians read—to describe how God breathed life into the first human: "God formed man, dust from the earth, and breathed into his face a breath of life, and the man became a living being" (Genesis 2:7 NETS). *Into* his face.

The same verb is used next when the prophet Elijah breathed into a dead widow's son, who had "no breath left in him" (1 Kings 17:17 NETS). Three times, Elijah breathed into the boy—restoring the Spirit-breath the boy had lost. *Into* the boy.

Again, the prophet Ezekiel describes how the storm of the Spirit-breath entered dead and dried bones, bleached in the sun, so that they rattled back to life (Ezekiel 37:9–10). *Into* the bones.

In each case, the Spirit-breath brings a body to life—or back to life. Adam, once dust, pulses with life. The widow's son, once dead, turns a mother's bereavement to delight. Israel, once a hopeless heap of bones, becomes a nation with a future. And now, in a locked room, Jesus breathes Spirit-breath *into* his exhausted and anxious friends.

Only the shock of intimacy can bring them back to life. So Jesus breathes *into*, not on, them the kiss of life. This is Jesus' legacy.

························

Knowing that *ruach* is Spirit-breath, *God's* breath in you, breathe in and out deeply for seven minutes at this, the start of week seven. (Set a timer, if need be.) As you breathe in, deeply and slowly, become aware of the ways in which your anxiety, worry and weariness cause you to be cut off from the world. Then spend your time simply resting. (No breathing exercises—just rest and relaxation.) Nearly seven minutes of pure rest. This is the kiss of life!

> *Holy Spirit,*
>> *Locked in a room*
>>> *anxious and exhausted*
>> *We see Jesus come to us*
>>> *breathe into us*
>> *Not from a distance*
>>> *standing aloof, remote*
>> *But with a kiss*
>>> *You come into us*
>> *And with you*
>> *renewal, purpose, joy. Amen.*

44

Teach and trust others

And He has put in his heart the ability to teach, in him and Aholiab the son of Ahisamach, of the tribe of Dan. He has filled them with skill to do all manner of work of the engraver and the designer and the tapestry maker, in blue, purple, and scarlet thread, and fine linen, and of the weaver—those who do every work and those who design artistic works.

—Exodus 35:34–35 NKJV

Remember chapter three, when we met artisans who crafted the high priest Aaron's Sunday best? These artisans were filled with the Spirit of wisdom, so they had the necessary skills—engraving, spinning, weaving, dying, woodworking—to build a wilderness tent for worship.

You may think they received those skills spontaneously, through a sudden filling with the Spirit. A wave of inspiration washing over them.

Maybe. But there's a better way to understand how they were filled with the Spirit of wisdom. The artisans in the desert reported to a chief artisan, Bezalel. God "filled him with the Spirit of God, in wisdom and understanding, in knowledge and all manner of workmanship, to design artistic works, to work in gold and silver and bronze, in cutting jewels for setting, in carving wood, and to work in all manner of artistic workmanship" (Exodus 35:31–33). Bezalel was an artisan. But, unlike other artisans, who were skilled in specific tasks, like building or dyeing or spinning, he was skilled in *every* kind of medium.

With so many skills, how did Bezalel lead? *By teaching.* That's exactly how the Bible reads here. God "put in his heart the ability to teach." Filled with the Spirit, with so many skills, so much knowledge, wisdom and understanding, what did Bezalel do? He left a legacy through teaching.

This little line, "put in his heart the ability to teach," tells us the artisans were filled with the Spirit, not through some overwhelming experience, but through the slow boil of learning. They were apprentices of Bezalel (and his sidekick, Aholiab), who had one job, and one job alone—to teach artisans, male and female, weavers and builders, the skills they needed to accomplish God's great work.

This is the school of the Spirit, where knowledge, wisdom and understanding are taught—and learned—skill by skill. Where filling with the Spirit happens stitch by careful stitch.

Where teaching matters. *Inspired* teaching, that is.

———

Take these moments today to do a few things. First, recall just one teacher, formal or informal, who inspired you. Next, focus on whatever skill you learned from this teacher. Finally, put a strategy in place to leave a legacy by teaching someone else that skill. Why? Because all of us learn to live the Spirit-filled life step by step, skill by skill, stitch by stitch.

> *Holy Spirit,*
>   *There's no shortcut to virtue*
>   *no quick fix for sin*
>   *no cutting-in-line to kindness*
>   *So let me learn slowly*
>   *Let me acquire wisdom—day by day*
>   *skills—step by step*
>   *understanding—mistake by mistake*
>   *And let me teach slowly, too*
>   *patiently explaining*
>   *humbly leading*
>   *kindly correcting*
>   *Enroll me as student and teacher—both*
>   *in the school of the Spirit. Amen.*

45

Learn to share responsibilities

Then the LORD said to Moses, "Gather for me seventy men of the elders of Israel, whom you know to be the elders of the people and officers over them, and bring them to the tent of meeting, and let them take their stand there with you. And I will come down and talk with you there. And I will take some of the Spirit that is on you and put it on them, and they shall bear the burden of the people with you, so that you may not bear it yourself alone."

—Numbers 11:16–17 ESV

Moses was an amazing leader, filled with so much of the Spirit that God distributed some of that Spirit to other people—many other people! But even Moses could be worn down by leadership, tattered by the demands of people in his charge.

That is where we find Moses today—at his wits' end, facing a mountain of civil lawsuits and complaints. And complaining himself. So God gave advice. And Moses listened.

The elders ventured out to the tent, where they would receive a portion of that Spirit to handle, with Moses, the responsibilities of leadership that rested on his shoulders alone. The elders were the beneficiaries of Moses' leadership.

But Moses was the beneficiary, too. Because he was willing to leave a legacy and share the authority of the Spirit, his load lifted. God told him straight up, "They shall bear the burden of the people with you, so that you may not bear it yourself alone."

Leaving a legacy means you don't have to bear your burden all alone. Sharing the Spirit, letting others work alongside you, benefits everyone. Good to know, right?

Moses apparently learned another lesson, as well. Later, two elders, Eldad and Medad, received the Spirit without going to the tent with the other elders. This violated God's command to "bring them to the tent of meeting." Moses' young right-hand man, Joshua, was flustered and frustrated by this breach, so he ordered Moses to tell Eldad and Medad, "Stop!"

Moses, a seasoned leader, learned that he couldn't control the legacy he left. So instead of constricting and curtailing, he embraced the oddities and eccentricities of those who received his legacy, and said to Joshua, "Are you jealous for my sake? Would that all the LORD's people were prophets, that the LORD would put his Spirit on them!" (Numbers 11:29).

Now, *that* perspective is a legacy worth leaving!

Yesterday, we thought about teachers, both formal and informal, who have left us a legacy. Today, think about the people who have received a legacy or mentorship of any sort from you. Take a few minutes to call or write to them—any sort of contact will do. In light of today's story of Eldad and Medad, express appreciation for the ways in which they have uniquely stretched, enlarged and even reshaped your legacy.

> *Holy Spirit,*
> > *Demands, demands and more demands*
> > *Life is sometimes one demand, one obligation, one task*
> > > *to do after another*
> > *And I'm exhausted—just like Moses*
> > *Inspire me to let go, to leave off, to surrender*
> > > *to let the student become the teacher*
> > > *to learn from those who've learned from me*
> > > *to let them bear my burdens*
> > > > *shoulder to shoulder—like the elders*
> > *Because there is more than enough of you to go around*
> > > *even in people where I might not expect to find*
> > > > *you—just like Eldad and Medad. Amen.*

46

Become a mentor

Now Joshua son of Nun was filled with the spirit of wisdom because Moses had laid his hands on him. So the Israelites listened to him and did what the LORD had commanded Moses.

—Deuteronomy 34:9 NIV

The laying on of hands was the final act of Moses' deep and enduring relationship with a young man named Joshua. You might say, in today's language, that Moses was Joshua's mentor, and Joshua was Moses' protégé.

When Joshua fought the Amalekites in a valley, Moses stood on the cliffs above, arms raised in prayer. Moses' arms grew so weary that they had to be held up—but hold them up he did (see Exodus 17:8–14).

When Moses climbed Mount Sinai, he left elders behind but took Joshua with him (see Exodus 24:12–14).

When Joshua wanted Eldad and Medad to stop prophesying, Moses replied instead, "I wish that all the LORD's people were prophets" (Numbers 11:29).

When Moses grew older, he designated Joshua the leader of the next generation (see Deuteronomy 31:7–8).

Moses prayed for Joshua. Moses took Joshua with him. Moses corrected Joshua. Moses commissioned Joshua. The laying on of hands, then, was just the final act of a lifelong relationship between a mentor and a protégé.

And what impact did that relationship have on Moses? You'll find out two verses earlier in Deuteronomy: "Moses was a hundred and twenty years old when he died, yet his eyes were not weak nor his strength gone" (34:7). Strength, lēḥō in Hebrew, really means freshness—fresh grapes rather than dried (Numbers 6:3), a green tree instead of brown (Ezekiel 17:24) and fresh cords used to tie Samson (Judges 16:7–8). Moses was still fresh enough to lay his hands on Joshua. That's why The Message reads, "His eyesight was sharp; he still walked with a spring in his step" (Deuteronomy 34:7).

This is a sparkling tribute to the power of leaving a legacy. After decades of discouragement and bouts of exhaustion, Moses still possessed a vitality he could pass on to Joshua. Moses was still fresh, still green, still alive, capable of passing, one last time, the Spirit of wisdom to his friend and faithful protégé.

Today, as you plan one errand or activity, think of one person younger or newer to the faith to take with you. Start building that relationship now so that when you, like Moses, are old (if you're not there already!), you'll still have a spring in your step.

> *Holy Spirit,*
>> *You've promised to be with me always*
>> *But that sense of your presence with me can become*
>>> *selfish*
>>> *self-centered*
>>> *self-seeking*
>> *So I pray you'll be with others through me*
>> *Give me the resolve to pray for someone else*
>>>> *to take someone else with me*
>>>> *to correct someone else who is*
>>>>> *fresher than I in the faith*
>> *And when the day comes, and I slow down to a crawl*
>> *I'll still have a spring in my slow step*
>>> *Still be fresh and full of life. Amen.*

47

Put your protégé to the test

Elijah said to Elisha, "Ask! What may I do for you, before I am taken away from you?" Elisha said, "Please let a double portion of your spirit be upon me." So he said, "You have asked a hard thing. Nevertheless, if you see me when I am taken from you, it shall be so for you; but if not, it shall not be so."

—2 Kings 2:9–10 NKJV

Elijah was a spectacular prophet. A man of miracles, Elijah multiplied grain and oil, raised a widow's son from the dead and predicted that the vindictive Israelite queen Jezebel would fall in a gruesome death. He was also known as a man of the Spirit. After he was taken up in a fiery chariot, those left behind wanted to search for him, so they asked Elijah's disciple, Elisha, if they could "go and search for your master, lest perhaps the Spirit of the LORD has taken him up and cast him upon some mountain or into some valley" (2 Kings 2:16). In death, as in life, Elijah was a man of the Spirit.

So it's no surprise that his disciple, Elisha, should ask for that same Spirit. What is surprising is that Elisha asked for a *double* portion of the Spirit that rested upon Elijah. This is an aggressive request. With his mentor facing death, Elisha didn't grieve or despair. He asked instead to be twice the prophet Elijah was.

It's a tough ask, and Elijah, his mentor, responded in kind, telling Elisha he'd receive a double portion of the Spirit only if Elisha saw him go. This might have been one last challenge, one final lesson to test the tenacity of Elijah's disciple.

If we have an idealized view of teacher and disciple, this story calls us up short. Elisha made an ambitious request just as Elijah was about to die. Elijah responded with a test of his own.

Clearly, the relationship between Elijah and Elisha wasn't cozy. It was strained by the waning of Elijah's influence and the waxing of Elisha's. There was little affection here.

But affection isn't the reason we leave a spiritual legacy. Inspiring the next generation is. And this happened. Elisha did see Elijah ascend in a fiery chariot and was off and running to more—and more impressive—miracles than even Elijah, a man of miracles, had managed.

The story of Elijah and Elisha tells us that leaving a spiritual legacy may require mentoring people with their own strong will. Today, identify a few younger men and women or Christians newer to the faith to lead the next generation—not just friendly or compatible ones, but ones with keen vision. Then pray for opportunities to initiate a conversation with one or more of them. Even if you don't continue in a mentoring relationship, your own vision of the future will expand by engaging with theirs. If you do continue in a mentoring relationship, you'll know from the start that their fresh vision of the future will challenge and keep you fresh, as well.

> *Holy Spirit,*
> *I pray for vision*
> *for wisdom*
> *knowledge*
> *understanding*
> *Teach me to receive that vision from others*
> *Others with a different vision*
> *with unusual wisdom*
> *knowledge*
> *understanding*
> *Challenge me to be not just a teacher—but a student*
> *not just a mentor—but a disciple*
> *not just an adult—but a child, too.*
> *Amen.*

48

Encourage the next generation

> For this reason I remind you to fan into flame the gift of
> God, which is in you through the laying on of my hands.
> For the Spirit God gave us does not make us timid, but
> gives us power, love and self-discipline.
>
> —2 Timothy 1:6–7 NIV

A little later in this letter, Paul, a mentor, wrote to a younger
protégé, Timothy, "And the things you have heard me say in
the presence of many witnesses entrust to reliable people
who will also be qualified to teach others" (2 Timothy 2:2).
That's four generations: Paul, Timothy, reliable people and
still others.

Four generations—an amazing vision of the power of leaving a legacy. But Paul was apparently well aware, too, of how easily this chain could be broken.

So Paul got down to the nitty-gritty of whether Timothy was up to the task of leading the next generation. What's stunning is how gently Paul did this. Even when he pushed Timothy to bold leadership, he did this gently, with encouragement rather than criticism.

Instead of, "You've let your faith die out," Paul told Timothy to fan into flame his gift. This verb, *fan into flame*, isn't weak. In the Greek Old Testament, Jacob's spirit fanned into flame—came to life—when he heard Joseph was still alive (Genesis 45:27). It's a strong verb—but an encouraging one, promising new life rather than condemning the old.

Paul also reminded Timothy that his spiritual gift came to Timothy through the laying on of Paul's hands: "I remind you to fan into flame the gift of God, which is in you through the laying on of my hands." This, too, is a tender reminiscence.

These are lines penned by a mentor, yes, but a friend, too, a father in the faith. To keep the chain strong, to make sure the Spirit of power, love and self-discipline would continue for generations to come, Paul prompted and prodded with genuine warmth and affection. He grasped the power of personal appeal, the lure of encouragement rather than criticism—the attraction, not of judgment, but of tenderness.

It's easy to criticize people younger in the faith—or just plain younger. As you think today about leaving a spiritual legacy, call to mind one criticism you may have lodged at younger Christians—or younger people in general. Begin your reflection by asking yourself whether such a criticism is even legitimate. Or is it simply a criticism of what is different? Or new? Or intimidating? Then, if you can still identify a worthwhile criticism, reframe it by making it positive. Transform a word of criticism into a tender word of encouragement. Then contact someone in the days ahead and express that generous and genuine word of encouragement in order to strengthen the chain of faith for generations to come.

> *Holy Spirit,*
> *You are the wellspring of a spiritual legacy*
>   *Not through judgment but inspiration*
>   *Not by criticism but encouragement*
>   *Not with severity but tenderness*
> *Because you are not the Spirit of scolding—but of*
>   *Power*
>   *exercised through*
>   *Love*
>   *by people of*
>   *Self-discipline*
>   *who curb criticism and cultivate kindness. Amen.*

49

Reflect on your spiritual legacy

I began this book by telling you about my first day in Jerry Hawthorne's Greek class at Wheaton College. I didn't tell you what happened later.

After my first year of graduate school at Duke University, Jerry invited me to teach his summer Greek class while he wrote a book on Paul's letter to the Philippians. He even invited me to live in his home with his family. At the start of each day, we'd hop into Jerry's old Volkswagen Beetle and chat about the day ahead. At day's end, I'd pop into Jerry's cubbyhole in the library to grapple over what he'd written that day.

The next summer, I lived again with Jane and Jerry Hawthorne while I taught intermediate Greek. Early one morning, I went downstairs. There was Jerry, sprawled on his knees, his face buried in the couch cushions, his Greek New Testament open at his right hand. He never even saw me.

Jerry, you can see, left me a spiritual legacy in both intentional and unplanned ways. His Spirit-filled life became a world in which I flourished.

We've glimpsed this week an array of Spirit-filled mentors. We've discovered that mentoring, however it occurs—training, teaching, testing, encouraging—is an essential dimension of the Spirit-filled life.

Today's photograph gives you the chance to reflect on your legacy. Jeremy and I visited a bird sanctuary, hoping for dramatic sunset photos. The sunset didn't materialize, but just as we were about to leave, we saw a roseate spoonbill fly by with a thatch of twigs in its bill. It was building a nest for the next generation. The day was nearly over, but the bird's work was not. Another generation was on the horizon.

This, then, is the seventh secret of the Spirit-filled life: *The Spirit-filled life is ours to live, yes, but just as importantly, ours to give. If we hope to flourish now, we must have one eye on what—on who—comes next.*

Pray for someone to mentor. Then invite that person to explore with you the possibility of a mentoring relationship. Don't force it. Let it grow naturally, remembering that mentors train, teach, test and encourage their protégés in a variety of ways inspired by the Holy Spirit.

Holy Spirit,
  Surveyor of the horizon
  Seeker of who's next
  Open my eyes to the next generation
                the nest generation. Amen.

ACKNOWLEDGMENTS

I have received generous financial support for this book from a variety of sources. The endowed chair that I hold at Perkins School of Theology, Southern Methodist University—the W. J. A. Power Chair of Old Testament Interpretation and Biblical Hebrew—underwrote the lion's share of travel required to curate photographs for this book. I received additional ample backing through a Scholarly Outreach Award from Perkins School of Theology. Finally, I completed this book as a guest professor at the Institutum Judaicum Delitzschianum, of the Westfälische Wilhelms-Universität, located in Münster, Germany, thanks to a resumption of my Alexander von Humboldt Fellowship. My host in Münster, Lutz Doering, arranged for Priscilla and me to have a sunlit office under the eaves, and his assistant, Frau Claudia Deimann, was instrumental in making arrangements for our pleasant two-month sojourn in this beautiful city.

I am especially grateful to the good people of Baker Publishing and Chosen Books. David Sluka has been an incomparable champion of this book, with its unique combination of written text and photographs. We spent hours in Zoom conversations hammering out titles for each week and day, and David has responded with dispatch and detail to every question I raised. On those occasions when he visited Dallas, we had the pleasure of a meal together. David's encouragement has been both heartfelt and heartening. Stephanie Smith and her team worked enthusiastically to produce and promote this book; with a spirit of collegiality, she solicited Jeremy's and my opinion on everything from book covers to subtitles. Christy Phillippe did an excellent job of copyediting the manuscript.

Rebecca Howdeshell, digital projects librarian in the special collections of the Bridwell Library at Southern Methodist University, twice made rare manuscripts available for Jeremy to photograph. Among the many splendors of the Bridwell, we opted for this Hebrew manuscript. Thanks also to Anthony Elia, the amiable and capable director of the library, and our friend, who tends the Bridwell's amazing resources. Thanks, too, are due to avid birders Phoebe Dishmann, Kathryn Walker and Rosine Hall, who pointed out great places in south Texas for photographs. Ted Campbell, my friend at Perkins School of Theology, connected me with these women.

This book has been a family affair. My son, Jeremy, for his part, proved to be the consummate professional. More than that, he was great fun, especially on the road, where we headed out before sunrise and then spent great days together, as we searched for the best photos to complement and cap off the devotionals for each week. I'm grateful for his goodwill; in Ennis, Texas, for example, he carried our yellow Formica table over a hundred yards to photograph it in a field of bluebonnets. On Bolivar beach, he set his tripod in knee-deep surf to photograph the sunrise. Then, when it came time for revision, my wife, Priscilla, research professor of practical theology at Perkins School of Theology, Southern Methodist University, closely read each devotional; in her usual way, her criticisms were laced with kindness, yet she never, for that reason, ignored the faults in my prose. Priscilla was not the only one to ply the trade of editor. Our daughter, Chloe, had a few months between completing her MBA and beginning a new job in Chicago, so she opted, I'm pleased to say, to join Priscilla and me in Münster. If Priscilla read the manuscript with the eyes of a trained theologian, Chloe read it through the keen eyes of an intelligent thirty-year-old woman with a flair for writing. My gratitude toward my family, then, is not perfunctory in the least. I am thrilled to say that this, genuinely, has been a family affair.

Internationally acclaimed scholar, award-winning author, and sought-after speaker **Jack Levison** (PhD, Duke University; MA, Cambridge University; BA, Wheaton College) is the W. J. A. Power Professor of Old Testament Interpretation and Biblical Hebrew at Southern Methodist University. Jack has the gift of connecting with popular audiences, with essays featured in the *Huffington Post*, parade.com, relevant.com and beliefnet.com, and he is renowned worldwide for his scholarship, with invitations to speak and research in Oxford, St. Andrews, Tübingen, Munich and Münster. Jack is the author of many books on the Holy Spirit, including *Fresh Air: The Holy Spirit for an Inspired Life*, *Forty Days with the Holy Spirit* and *An Unconventional God: The Spirit according to Jesus*. *A Boundless God: The Spirit according to the Old Testament* was chosen by *Christianity Today* as a 2021 Award of Merit winner, with these words: "Who knew that a word study could read like an adventure story—welcome to the world of the Holy Spirit in the Old Testament." Jack's life is, in fact, an adventure. He and his wife, Priscilla, both professors at SMU, live with two hundred students as faculty-in-residence in Boaz Commons on the SMU campus. Quite the adventure!

Jeremy Pope-Levison (BA, Southern Methodist University) is a freelance photographer and videographer. He and his wife, Miranda, make their home in Dallas, Texas. Learn more at levisonmediagroup.com.